W9-CEW-696

To Be or Wanna Be

The Top Ten Differences Between a Successful Actor and a Starving Artist

To Be or *Wanna* Be

The Top Ten Differences Between a Successful Actor and a Starving Artist
by Sean Pratt

Jim —

Bang Your Own Drum!

Sean Pratt

CreateSpace.com

To Be or Wanna Be: The Top 10 Differences Between a Sucessful Actor and a Starving Artist © Sean Pratt, 2012
Published by Sean Pratt Presents.

ISBN-13:978-1477597880
ISBN-10:1477597883

All rights reserved. No part of this publication may be reproduced, stored in a retrieval system or transmitted in any form or by any means without the prior written permission of the publisher.

Cover Photography by Bigstock.com, DC Cathro. Back cover author photo by Clinton Brandhagen / clintonbrandhagenphotography.com.

FIRST PRINTING

Acknowledgements
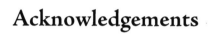

ACKNOWLEDGEMENTS

No book, or any big project, really, is created by just one person. When I work on any new aspect of Sean Pratt Presents, and am searching for people to collaborate with, enthusiasm is the main quality I look for, along with intelligence and insight. I love being around people who view excellence as a way of being and not something to occasionally strive for. That said, I want to thank my mother, Sandra Pratt, for patiently editing the articles, notes, and scribblings that were the pieces which became this book; my wife, Shannon, for inspiring me to write it and challenging my ideas when she thought they weren't clear enough; my editor, Heather Benjamin, for doing a great job cleaning up my prose; Shelby Sours, for collaborating on the teaching syllabus; DC Cathro, for creating such a delightful cover; John McElroy, for helping produce the audiobook version of this little tome; Amber Spence, for all her work at keeping my presence on the web up to date; and finally, to all the actors who have spent their evenings and weekends at my workshops, classes, and coaching sessions. You graciously gave your time and allowed me to road-test my ideas and hone them into these ten crucial differences. Thank you all!

For Mom and Dad, who taught me how,

For Shep and Joanne, who showed me how,

For the actors, who ask me how,

For Shannon, who makes it all worthwhile.

Table of Contents

Introduction

INTRODUCTION

Being labeled a "successful actor" is something at once subjective and objective, personal and public. It is subjective and personal in that actors must learn to create their own yardstick by which they measure their success, usually from setting specific goals and keeping track of how far along they are in achieving them. Yet there are certain objective standards that can be applied to all actors and their efforts. These universal standards become the gauge by which actors are deemed to be failing or succeeding in their careers by the public at large, as well as by those who know and work with them personally.

To illustrate this, I've highlighted the ten behaviors, actions, or attitudes that have the greatest effect on an actor's chances of success. I contrast these positive behaviors, attitudes, and actions with the destructive ones, starting with the core differences and expanding to encompass the more complex ones. I thought long and hard about the mind-set I've tried to create in my own career, and also observed in others, that allows actors to develop a strong network of friends and colleagues in "the Biz," to keep building on each small achievement they earn, and to stay focused on the goals they have yet to accomplish.

I'll be the first to say that, though I wish I was the wise "Show-Biz Buddha," perfectly balanced and master of all these differences, I'm not! It seems that as soon as I chart some progress in one of the ten areas, I catch myself coming up short in another. But I've been practicing these behaviors long enough to know that they do provide me with real benefits and measurable successes. In each chapter, I'll be sharing a personal story of how I came to discover this key difference or the way I use it in my career today. No matter where you are on your career path, understanding these differences can be of great value to you. From the raw beginner to the seasoned pro, there will be ideas and actions listed here that can give you a new perspective or a gentle reminder of what it takes to be a successful actor.

Now this isn't just a book you read and ponder, it's about something you do! To get the true value of what my little treatise is offering, you must think of it as a call to action and a "how-to" manual for your career in the Biz. That's why I've included a section at the end of every chapter titled "So... Let's Get Started!" Here, you'll find specific, concrete steps you can take to begin working toward the concept or attitude discussed in that chapter. Also, I've thrown in a selection of books for further reading that relate to that particular topic.

TO BE OR WANNA BE

After reading this book, choose a few of the differences to focus on and begin to practice them ASAP! If you do, I promise you'll soon begin to see their positive effects, making your life and career something to look forward to and not to dread! No matter whether you currently think of yourself as the "starving artist" who feels that her career is going nowhere fast or the actor who's already racing up the ladder of success, there's something in here for you to think about and to do.

Actions, thoughts, and behavior are a choice… just like acting. Choosing to change the way you've been doing things is the first step in creating a life and career that will lead to more fulfillment and success. Everybody starts out as a starving artist. But as you learn to recognize the differences between a positive and a destructive mind-set, you'll begin to see the changes in your career that will lead you from success to success. Not to sound too clichéd here, but I do want to remind you that success is not a destination, but a process; it's the journey to the top of the mountain, not the single goal of reaching the summit, that matters. The challenges you face along the way, the confidence you build in overcoming them, and the satisfaction you get from those small victories — these are the things that create success in your career. Always take the time to acknowledge your victories, however great or small they may be. Even if you only did one thing today that related to moving your career forward, allow yourself the happiness that comes from knowing that you completed that task. That one thing has moved you that much further down the road to becoming a successful actor!

So read this book often, practice it daily, and keep it for forever… or maybe, just maybe, one day you can pass it on to some young starving artist who's looking for a way to travel up that magic ladder of success.

Sean Pratt
June 2012

A Note on Terminology

A NOTE ON TERMINOLOGY

Choosing the term "successful actor" as the positive label to put on these behaviors was pretty easy. The first word connotes a happy, motivated, and profitable state of being, and the second word defines its vocation. But coming up with the right label for the opposite of that was a little tricky—Newbie? Loser? None sounded right. Then my wife Shannon suggested "starving artist," and I knew that was it. For me, this term conjures up the driven, intelligent actor whose career is struggling along, not from a lack of trying, but because he just doesn't have the business acumen or life experience necessary to guide him toward his goals. We all start out as starving artists, we all know what it feels like, and we all know we don't want to be one forever.

When I use an illustrative example or refer to the actions of a successful actor or starving artist, as much possible, I have decided to avoid using the awkward use of dual pronouns; his or her, he or she, himself or herself, and so on. I know that using these inclusive pronouns is considered proper form, as my mother Sandra, a secretary of fifty years, has repeatedly told me, but they're so clunky, and read so much like a government report, that I couldn't bear it. Sorry, mom. So instead, I'll be using the plural forms of the pronouns, or I'll choose a gender at random when referring to someone; simply, him or her. So... let's get started!

Difference #1
A Successful Actor takes responsibility for his career.
A Starving Artist looks for someone to blame.

Whatever happens, take responsibility.

—Tony Robbins

DIFFERENCE #1

One of the first things I say to an actor at the start of a coaching session is "Congratulations! You're taking responsibility for your career." The first step in becoming a successful actor is to hold yourself accountable for your actions. We live in an unpredictable world, and events occur that are frankly beyond our control. Yet at the same time, we have a career to pursue and a life to live. Now to deal with this unpredictability, you can adopt one of two mind-sets. One is "proactive"; the other is "no-active." You'll notice I didn't say "reactive," because I think of being reactive as a consequence of a "no-active" mind-set.

You see, the act of not choosing to do anything is itself a choice. This is because there's one factor surrounding any given choice which will inevitably change... time. Eventually, time will move on and the window for making a particular choice will close—and a different choice, or set of choices, will present itself.

Now, although there are some times in life where taking no action and allowing things to progress without interference is the right thing to do, the same cannot be said when it comes to the Biz. The play must be cast, the set must be built, and the show must go on! Delaying action, in those situations, is destructive to the creative process and by extension to your acting career.

It's easy to understand why actors might feel they have no control over their career and adopt a no-active mind-set. We work in a business that has no formal structure in place to review our efforts and reward us accordingly. There is no board that meets once a year to hand out promotions, no employee manual that tells us about a guaranteed raise after x number of years. Not only that, but because most acting schools focus on the "show" part of show business, an actor starts her career having no clue about where to begin, who to trust, and how to measure her progress. But whether we call it procrastination, indecision, or stonewalling, this no-active mindset leads to a passive state of victimhood... and a victim needs someone to blame.

"My agent isn't getting me any work." "My manager won't return my phone calls." "That casting director must hate me, because she never calls me in for auditions." "If only this or that had happened, my career would be perfect!" Oh, the soothing feeling of self-pity. For a short time, it chases away the worry and self-doubt. It lets you give full vent to the conspiracy theories of why your career is being sabotaged and by whom. Living in fear is the natural consequence of the no-active mind-set.

Starving artists live in fear and claim victimhood; successful actors confront their fears by being proactive and claiming responsibility.

The Subway Cowboy

The moment when I first took full responsibility for my career came when I was a student at drama school. Along with 30 other college actors, I journeyed to London to attend fall classes at the British American Drama Academy. This was my senior semester abroad from the College of Santa Fe in New Mexico, where I was working toward my BFA in acting. Like many of the other students, I had scrimped and saved all summer — waiting tables, painting houses, and doing odd jobs — and was thrilled to be traveling abroad for the first time to have the opportunity of training with these wonderful teachers in England.

My excitement was short-lived, however. I realized that after using all my scholarships and savings, along with the money my folks had been able to spare, to pay for the classes and a room at a student hostel, I was left with a grand total of $300 to live on for the next five months.

When I was growing up, my father had constantly said to me, "Always have a Plan B. You never know when Plan A is going to blow up in your face." But here I was, practically broke and without a clue as to how I would come up with a Plan B. I couldn't work as a waiter without a permit, I couldn't ask my folks for any more money, and if I didn't come up with something soon, I was going to end up catching a flight back home.

So how badly did I want to be an actor, anyway? Was it worth this? Was the vague promise of future success important enough to put up with this very real hardship in the here and now? Was I really willing to take responsibility for choosing this career and then do whatever was necessary to succeed at it?

The answer to my problem came a few days later. I was going down to the Tube when I saw a man playing his guitar at the bottom of the escalator. He was singing, in a very strong Scottish brogue, a Country and Western tune; it was sort of a "Fat Bastard sings Hank Williams." As I passed by, I looked down at his guitar case and saw that it was full of money! Now, in the time-honored tradition of young college actors everywhere, I had been playing folk guitar from the age of 14—my inspiration being mainly to meet girls. Luckily, I had brought my guitar to London with just this purpose in mind, but now realized it was to be the instrument of my salvation...so to speak.

So, every weekend, I would put on my boots, jeans, and Western shirt and journey down to my spot at the Oxford Circus station to sing and play to the passersby. I'd make enough to eat on and have a little pocket money for the rest of the week. I did that for the next five months.

Some student actors, when they hear me tell this story, say, "How cool! Living the life of an artist on the edge and making it happen!" But there was very little about it that was cool, or even fun...especially when the weather turned colder and my fingers would go numb or my voice would get tired from singing. What I tell them is that was the moment when I walked across a line in the sand—that dividing line which separates those who take responsibility for their careers from those who don't. That experience changed me in so many ways; it forced me to confront a whole host of fears, to realize how strong I really was, and to take my work as an actor seriously.

I Know What I Know

Successful actors understand that life is uncertain and that even their best-laid plans can go awry. Nevertheless, they know that the only way to lessen the effect of those mistakes and keep the odds in their favor is to be proactive. Being proactive forces them to think, thinking leads them to a decision, their decision leads to action, and in the moment that they act, they take responsibility for their career.

One of the biggest decisions successful actors make is to have faith in themselves and faith that their actions will lead to positive outcomes that change their circumstances for the better. We know that our circumstances are just the manifestation of our choices writ large. Because starving artists live in fear, they feel they have few choices or that others are supposed to be making the choices for them. Successful actors, benefiting from the self-confidence that responsibility gives them, see limitless choices. This reveals itself in many areas of their career.

When it comes to looking at their careers in general, successful actors have accepted the fact that they are at once the CEO and the secretary, the head of marketing and the mailroom clerk of "My Acting Career, Inc." Once they make that choice, they take responsibility for it. They make the decisions as to where they'll spend their time and resources, as well as what kind of work they want to do and where they want to do it. Successful actors own up to the fact that it's essential to understand not only the artistic aspects of their career, but also the marketing, financial, and networking aspects.

Successful actors know that even though an agent, casting director, or producer may present them with opportunities, it's their responsibility to prepare for them, seize them when they arrive, and see them through to completion. As an agent once said to me, "Sean, the harder you work on your end, the easier it is for me to open doors for you." Successful actors refuse to blame their circumstances on others, knowing that their own career choices determine their circumstances and not the other way around. Yes, of course the universe is going to throw obstacles in your way that you have no control over, that you didn't deserve, and that seem to sabotage your best efforts to move forward. The challenge is to figure out what aspects of these things you can control, focus on them, and try your best not to worry about the things outside your control. It's not an easy task, but one you must strive for, because to worry about those uncontrollable elements leads to a "no-active" mind-set. As long as you complain about your career, you are taking a "no-active" approach to it, refusing to own it, and allowing time (through inaction) or someone else (through inattention) to make your decisions for you.

So remember:
A Starving Artist looks for someone to blame.
A Successful Actor takes responsibility for his career.

DIFFERENCE #1

So... Let's Get Started!

Here are some practical steps for achieving the goal of taking responsibility for your career. Use them as a framework from which you can build your own personalized method and new mindset.

1. Start off with this little mantra; I've used it for years: "This is my career and no one else's. How far I go and how high I climb is totally up to me. Though I will seek out the help, advice, and guidance of those around me, I will never blame anyone for my lack of success or any setbacks that may occur. I will never measure my success by someone else's yardstick, but by the goals I set for myself and how well I attain them. So, what can I do today that will move my career forward?"

2. Find a quiet place to do some thinking. Ask yourself, is there some aspect of your career that you've been taking a "no-active" approach to? Are you afraid of trying to push yourself for fear of failing? Self-awareness is the first step in overcoming this paralyzing mind-set. Start small and write down just two or three things you know you've been avoiding or are blaming someone else for. For example:

   • Are you blaming your agent or manager for not finding you work?

   • Do you feel overwhelmed by all the "hats" you have to wear and things you need to do to run "Your Acting Career, Inc."?

   • Do you doubt your talent, beauty, or knowledge?

   • Is it easier to envy another actor's success than to learn from your own setbacks?

   • Are you constantly looking for new opportunities or letting them slip away because of a lack of discipline?

3. Once you've identified these problem areas, you must try your best to do the following:

   • Make a conscious effort to stop the negative internal dialogue that's running in your head, the one that blames others or finds excuses for your no-active behavior. Listen to how you frame a problem when talking about it. The pattern of blaming others or your circumstances is part of this destructive mind-set. If you can hear it, then you can stop it. When dealing with my own issues, I literally say out loud, "Nope. Stop that! This is my problem to solve."

- As you begin to own your career-related problems, you will naturally start to become proactive. Being proactive will force you to think about possible solutions, that thinking will lead you to a moment of decision, that decision will lead you to take action, and in the moment that you act, you'll begin to take responsibility for your career.

- Keep a journal or diary of your efforts in order to have a quantifiable record of your achievements. For me, my daily planner is where I record the goals I set for myself, as well as my thoughts on how I'm doing, day in and day out.

For Further Reading

- *Little Book of YES! Attitude: How to Find, Build and Keep a YES! Attitude for a Lifetime of Success* by Jeffrey Gitomer

- *TheSeven Spiritual Laws of Success: A Practical Guide to the Fulfillment of Your Dreams* by Deepak Chopra

- *7 Secrets for Successful Living: Tapping the Wisdom of Ralph Waldo Emerson to Achieve Love, Happiness, and Self-Reliance* by Marianne Parady

- *Acting: Make It Your Business—How to Avoid Mistakes and Achieve Success as a Working Actor* by Paul Russell

Difference #2
A Successful Actor pursues excellence.
A Starving Artist is satisfied with mediocrity.

Be a yardstick of quality. Some people aren't used to an environment where excellence is expected.

—Steve Jobs

How good is good enough? When is the best you have "the best there is?" And can it be better today than it was yesterday? Is perfection really attainable, and what if you seem to always come up short when you try for it? Do you feel embarrassed when you make the effort to tell others about your accomplishments? Does practice really make perfect?

Successful actors know that what was good the day before is no longer good enough today. One of the hardest things to watch is an actor who has allowed his talents to atrophy. He was deemed good or even excellent at one point in his career, but then he chose to just coast along at that level and not try to refine or expand his talents. Then he's in danger of becoming a starving artist again.

You must always push yourself to do better, knowing all the while that perfection is just an ideal. Plato's responsible for this one; it's his fault for giving us the concept in the first place! A more realistic idea or goal is called "the pursuit of excellence," and the successful actor achieves it in two ways: the first is by doing something called "deliberate practice"; the second is by overcoming the three big obstacles that prevent starving artists from promoting themselves in the Biz. Let's look at them one at a time.

Deliberate Practice

"Deliberate practice" is a phrase coined by the Swedish psychologist Dr. K. Anders Ericsson. His research revealed that though it may appear that excellence is achieved from years of daily practice, not just any kind of practice will result in excellence. In fact, when most people practice something, they focus on the things they already know how to do. Playing the scales on the piano, running your lines over and over again, tackling the same kind of project you worked on the week before—all these are examples of regular practice.

Instead, to become successful at any pursuit, you must focus your efforts on some specific aspect of your craft that you can't do well or even do at all; that is deliberate practice. It's only by exerting yourself in this way, with its emphasis on new challenges and attention to detail, that you will broaden and deepen your abilities and find yourself becoming exceptional at them.

Think about all those times you had to focus on learning something new, difficult, and challenging as an actor, something at which you had to succeed if you wanted to move forward in your career. The days spent rehearsing a dance number for a musical, the hundreds of hours spent talking into a microphone to learn how to become an audiobook narrator, the endless takes in front of the camera when shooting a video or film—initially, all of these were things you had never done before and were not very good at doing. But those grueling hours spent pushing yourself physically and mentally taught you two important things when it comes to practicing your craft. To quote Dr. Ericsson, "Deliberate practice involves two kinds of learning: improving the skills you already have and extending the reach and the range of your skills." (Ericsson, Krampe, & Tesch-Romer, 1993). So it seems that ordinary practice does not make you perfect, it just makes you passable; but deliberate practice turns you from a novice into an expert.

The Road to Kansas City

The first time I ran up against the concept and challenge of what Dr. Ericsson would come to label "deliberate practice" was the first play I did in college. During freshman year, I attended Southwestern Oklahoma State University in Weatherford. The musical for that season was—you guessed it!—Rogers and Hammerstein's Oklahoma! (There's a joke back home to the effect that if you want to be a professional actor, you're not allowed to leave the state until you've performed in this show.)

When auditions were announced, I set my sights on playing Will Parker. I had done some musicals in high school, and thought I stood a pretty good chance at landing this particular role. But when the cast list was finally posted, I saw that I would be playing the chorus role of Cowboy #3. The director pulled me aside, saying, "Sean, I really wish you could sing and dance better." Well, such is the lot of many a freshman actor, so I decided to chalk this one up to a "learning experience" and started going to rehearsals.

Three weeks later, fate intervened. I got a call from the stage manager on a Saturday morning and was told to hightail it down to the theatre. Brad, the music major who had been cast as Will, had undergone emergency surgery for a burst appendix and was out of the show for good. When I arrived at the theatre, the director, choreographer, and music director proceeded to put me through the most stressful audition I have ever experienced! After running me ragged for a solid hour, the consensus was, "Well, I guess Sean will have to do." And so I was recast as Will Parker, albeit with little fanfare.

DIFFERENCE #2

But don't think I was jumping up and down over my promotion. During the previous several weeks, I had watched Brad struggle with the central challenge of the role: the character's solo number, "Kansas City." In the hands of a Broadway pro, this song, and its extended dance sequence, would give the actor a chance at a real star turn, but for a 19-year-old kid with only a little singing and dancing under his belt, it could very well turn into a nightmare.

As Ericsson would say, the real challenge facing me was to improve the skills I already had and to extend the reach of my skills in order to pull this off in the two remaining weeks of rehearsal. I spent hours and hours and hours focusing on that one number. I never knew my feet could be so sore from dancing in cowboy boots or how much skill it takes to sing in full voice while doing it...but I learned. The hardest part was that it didn't all come together for me until right before the show opened. I had to trust that all this effort was going to be worth it in the end and that my parents wouldn't have to pretend they didn't know me after they saw the show.

But come together it did! When the director walked up to me at the cast party and said, "I can't tell you how happy I am that you proved us all wrong. That was one of the best damn Will Parkers I've ever seen!," I was speechless.

Yet the biggest payoff from that experience was what it did for me during the rest of my college years. I built on that work and pushed myself further to play even harder roles, like the dentist in Little Shop of Horrors and Kenickie in Grease. By demanding that I transcend the level of talent and skill I possessed, I earned one of the greatest gifts any performer can have—the self-confidence to know that I could meet any challenge that was thrown at me.

The Big Three

But all the deliberate practice in the world will do you no good if you don't feel comfortable showing or sharing it with directors, agents, and producers. You have to find work in order to put your practice to the test, and that means promoting yourself. So when it comes to advancing your career, generating interest in your projects, and calling attention to your unique abilities, you must realize that you're faced with three common obstacles.

These impediments are: what our society teaches us about the idea of calling attention to ourselves, the ill-informed mistakes actors make when they begin to market themselves, and the insidious effects of "groupthink." But don't despair, there's an answer to each of these problems.

Banging Your Own Drum

In childhood, we were told that showing off was uncouth, arrogant, and prideful. We were taught that to crow over our attributes and accomplishments was simply wrong. But while our parents were right in a general sense about boasting, perhaps we failed to understand an important exception to the rule— promotion and advertising are essential to the success of any business, and the product and service you are promoting... is you!

The first and most important adjustment to make toward becoming a successful actor is getting over your feelings of guilt, apprehension, and fear about promoting yourself. The ability to step outside yourself and your ego, to look at your talents and achievements with an eye for using them as stepping stones to something better, is essential. If you're an actor, then act like a marketing director! This is where seeking out expert advice can be critical, either from a business coach, taking Biz-related classes in marketing, or simply immersing yourself in the many books, videos, and articles available on the topic.

The Learning Curve

Another hurdle to overcome is your own naiveté and inexperience at the subtle art of self-promotion. There is a fine line between promoting your work in an engaging and informative way and being heavy-handed and boorish. You may be one of the most sophisticated, intelligent, and talented actors around, but telling everyone this, without a trace of modesty or charm, is neither sophisticated nor intelligent.

The best praise you can have is from a third party. A great review, a glowing letter of recommendation, or praise from your colleagues and peers can have a very positive affect on the reader and may even be the tipping point that causes them to call you in for that audition. When included in a review sheet or a cover letter, they will give credibility and legitimacy to your efforts at self-promotion.

Groupthink

The last major barrier for you to overcome is a phenomenon that sociologists have studied for a long time. Within any group, be it students in a classroom or workers on the factory floor, there can exist an expectation to achieve a certain level of success and no more. Those who try to shoot for something higher, meaning better grades or faster production, are kept in line through peer pressure... those who stand out, stand alone.

If you find yourself hanging out in a circle of starving artists who all seem to be content in their world of struggling to jumpstart their careers while complaining about their day jobs and commiserating about their fate, then you need to realize something. The potential for your future success far outweighs the comfort you now feel with being "in the group." In fact, it may be time to expand your circle of friends to include those successful actors who are just as driven as you are and who will inspire you, through their actions and peer pressure, to achieve more.

They say that you must have a thick skin in order to survive in this business, but not enough consideration is given to these inner conflicts and their ability to create roadblocks to your success. Ultimately, you must break through and resolve these issues in order to create and maintain the focus you need to not only pursue excellence, but also to promote your career.

So remember:
A Starving Artist is satisfied with mediocrity.
A Successful Actor pursues excellence.

So... Let's Get Started!

But how do successful actors translate their practice into a performance of sustained quality? How do they set, measure, and maintain a standard that allows them say, "I am pursuing and achieving excellence in my work?" Some actors write down their thoughts or impressions in a journal or diary, but without some kind of structured method, their observations can lack focus. Without focus, there can be no clarity of analysis and no way to truly learn from the experience. This is the fate that befalls the starving artist.

I want to share with you the approach I use to pursue excellence in my work. I call it the "Plan, Act, Reflect" method.

Plan

Before the project begins, you must do three things—set very clear goals for yourself, create a yardstick to measure your success and growth, and fashion a detailed plan of action. Let's use the example of you playing a lead role in an upcoming musical-comedy production. Let's choose one big issue to focus on, such as the vocal challenges of playing this role. Here's what you might be thinking about:

• The goal—to maintain my vocal strength throughout the entire run of the show.

• The yardstick—not losing my voice due to fatigue, overexertion, or illness.

• The plan—to start working with a voice coach, be aware of vocal strain during rehearsals and performance, and get plenty of rest.

Act

Now you're ready for rehearsals to begin, but you must also monitor what's happening to you; you're setting up a feedback loop. Specificity is important here. The more detailed the observations you make, the better you can adjust the direction of your performance in relation to your goal. For instance:

• "I don't have the stamina to get through the big dance number. I'm really out of breath. Perhaps I need to scale back on going to the gym every morning before rehearsal."

• "It's really dry in the dressing room. I'll ask the other actors if I can bring in a humidifier."

• "I'm straining during the last phrase of my big solo. I've got to work with my coach on this."

Reflect

Take time, after opening night, to review your notes, evaluate what is working and what isn't, and continue to challenge yourself throughout the run of the show. You can do this by creating a new plan to deal with any problems that come up. There will always be problems; what counts is your reaction to them. Remember to focus, in detail, on what you can control instead what you can't. For example:

• "I need to ask the costumer to adjust my Act One outfit. It's not staying on correctly and it's distracting me during my first song."

• "I've got to find a place to catnap between shows on the weekend in order to rest my voice."

• "I'm still not comfortable with my Act Three song because of the changes in blocking and the new props. I'll need to rehearse that scene a few times before tomorrow's show."

Finally, when the show closes, take a little time to go over the whole experience in relation to how you dealt with the challenge of that one particular issue. Where did you succeed? What could you have done differently? What were the unique circumstances of this show that either helped you or created roadblocks? And last, how will you use this experience to make your next performance even better?

For Further Reading

• *Human Accomplishment: The Pursuit of Excellence in the Arts and Sciences, 800 B.C. to 1950* by Charles Murray

• *The 7 Habits of Highly Effective People* by Stephen Covey

Difference #3
A Successful Actor has the right day job.
A Starving Artist takes any job
that comes along.

Artists spend 75% of their time working at something that lets them do their art the other 25% of the time, if they're fortunate!

—Sylvia Sleigh

DIFFERENCE #3

When I sit down with an actor for a career coaching session, one of the first questions I ask is, "What's your day job, and will it support all the career goals you want to achieve?" Successful actors quickly figure out that the kind of day job they choose has a direct effect on their chances of having a prosperous acting career. If need be, they develop additional skills that give them more latitude when looking for a day job and generate more opportunities for finding the right fit for their needs.

On the other hand, starving artists, desperate for any job that will pay the bills, usually end up in a line of work that not only keeps them "just getting by" financially, but also ends up sabotaging their career goals. They realize, too late, that they've trapped themselves in a no-win situation. They can't afford to take off for auditions and shows, because they don't earn enough money to make up for the lost work time, much less invest in their career. It becomes a destructive catch-22!

This conundrum of finding the right day job is best visualized as a three-legged stool. One leg represents earning the most money possible per hour of work. The second leg represents having the flexibility, during work hours, to take off and go to auditions, interviews, callbacks, and so on. Finally, the last leg represents having a job that allows you to either work when you want to, or come back to the job after the project is finished and pick up where you left off. Remove any one leg from the stool and it won't stand—and your acting career will end up toppling over. Of course, it almost goes without saying that besides these three important issues, you should look for a day job that brings you some level of personal fulfillment. Since you know that your ultimate day job is to work as an actor, try to find something that at least, in the meantime, engages or challenges you.

To find the day job that best fits these three requirements takes some ingenuity and effort. But successful actors are both smart and curious and willing to be creative in their day job search. They don't limit themselves to just waiting tables or working as a temp for hire, even though these do meet the basic test of the three-legged stool. Starving artists fall into these kinds of jobs simply because other actors are doing them or they think that anything more sophisticated will demand too much of their time and end up stifling their career. This is simply not so.

TO BE OR WANNA BE

If I Had a Hammer...

My father was a full-time firefighter with the Oklahoma City Fire Department, but he ran a small house-painting business on the side. As soon as my brother Curt and I were old enough, we joined him on jobs during the summer. Here I learned how to paint, glaze windows, and do basic carpentry repair. Though we worked hard, learned a lot, and made a little money, I think Dad barely broke even with us on the job, because he always picked up the lunch tab. Maybe that's why we always ate at the local cafeteria.

During my time at the College of Santa Fe, I landed one of those coveted work-study positions in the theatre scene shop. There I picked up a whole host of skills from our technical director: welding, drawing and reading blueprints, basic wiring, creative problem solving, and the motto, "A clean shop is a happy shop." During my college summers, I worked as a framing carpenter, sweating on a hot concrete slab from morning 'til night throwing up stud walls and roofing joists. Grueling work, but it paid very well.

Ironically, I didn't really think about what I would be doing for a day job once I left school. I just assumed that my brilliant talent would be immediately recognized and it would be off to Broadway for instant fame and fortune. I now chalk this up to being 21 and dumb as a post about the realities of the Biz. Needless to say, upon graduating, I was a bit flummoxed about how I was going to pay the bills while looking for acting work.

I had dabbled in other kinds of jobs as a teenager—record store clerk, barback, short-order cook, personal assistant to a public relations guy, even playing in a rock and roll band—but now I was having trouble finding a day job that satisfied those three important conditions of money, flexibility, and control. For a while, I thought waiting tables would do the trick, so I got a job at a groovy local restaurant, and though I made good money and it was pretty flexible, I found that the job itself was ultimately unsatisfying. All I had to show for my work at the end of my shift was a handful of cash and sweaty, dirty clothes. There had to be something better.

While puzzling over what to do next, I got a call from a friend. "You told me you do painting and carpentry, right? Well, my mother needs some work done around her place. Want a job?" I was at her house the following Monday. My five days of work there turned into a regular gig as her gardener/handyman.

Then I picked up two of her friends as clients, as well. Add to that the days spent remodeling houses, either on my own or as part of a crew, and I had a full-time job doing part-time work.

By this time, I realized I had found my perfect day job! First off, being a carpenter/painter/gardener paid great money, and because I worked hard and was reliable, I always had repeat business or referrals. Since the work was episodic, one day here or one week there, I could schedule it around my auditions. Finally, because I took on the extra responsibility of being my own boss, I could decide if and when to take work while doing a show or film. One bonus was that always searching for more of this work, with its required following up of leads, negotiating with potential clients, and being totally responsible for the outcome of the job, translated nicely into the business skills required for me to become a successful actor.

When I moved to New York City a few years later, I brought all this experience with me. I truly did a little of everything: made crates for an art shipping company, built at least a hundred lofts and bookcases, painted apartments on Fifth Avenue, and even built sets for Playwrights Horizons and the New York Public Theatre (NYPT).

Now is being a carpenter or painter the answer to every actor's day job dilemma? No, of course not. But finding a day job that gave me a good paycheck, the flexibility to audition at a moment's notice, and enough freedom to work when I needed to may just have been the difference between my becoming a successful actor or remaining a starving artist.

Perhaps you already have a day job, but sense that it's not the right one. Well, if you haven't gone to a single interview, taken an acting class, or gone to one audition in the last month because of your day job, ask yourself, "Did I come all this way and put up with all this hardship to end up being tied to a day job that's holding me back from pursuing my dreams?" If the answer is "No," then it's time to start looking for a new day job.

The first question you should be asking yourself is, "What skills do I possess that I could use to create a job where I have more, if not total control over my work schedule?" There are many potential day jobs where you could be in business for yourself and set your own hours, such as a massage therapist, gardener, or freelance salesman, to name but a few. You may not be able to find work that lets you be the boss of your own time right away. It may take months or sometimes even years to build the skills and experience necessary to be able to pick and choose among job opportunities, but hang in there. Once you reach the point of being able to make your own schedule, your freedom to seek work as an actor will exponentially increase.

Acting IS My Day Job

Now let's turn to what I consider to be the best kind of day job: the one that uses your skills as an actor. All too often, actors are so focused on traveling down one path to achieving their goals that they turn a blind eye to other kinds of acting work and never see what's on the periphery. The truth is that very few actors ever make a living by working in only one venue, and beyond that, many find that the experience of working in a different setting gives them new insights and abilities. These new skills will ultimately make them better actors.

Many actors view theatre, film, or TV as the only legitimate outlets and opportunities for work. They don't see trade shows, training videos, commercial modeling, and so forth as being worthy of their time and talent. While these projects may not be artistically satisfying, they certainly can be technically challenging if you make them so. As the saying goes, "If you're bored, you must be boring." Truly, the smart, curious, and driven actor can take any project and turn it into a rewarding experience.

So when the chance comes along to do something different from your usual work as an actor, something that would demand more of you as both an artist and a professional, seize it! The director of that training video you work on could be the one who hires you for her indie film. The money you make as the spokesperson for a company at their tradeshow will pay your rent while you're working at a summer stock theatre playing Hamlet. The infomercial you host could give you the experience you need to land that cable TV show you've dreamed of. The path to your ultimate success does not travel in a straight line, but is full of twists and turns...so, are you ready to start taking advantage of all the opportunities that will come your way?

So remember:
A Starving Artist takes any job that comes along.
A Successful Actor has the right day job.

DIFFERENCE #3

So... Let's Get Started!

To give you a kick start, here is a short list of day jobs, other than waiting tables or retail sales, that actors often find themselves doing:

- Carpentry or any of the construction trades
- Legal proofreading
- Temp work or telemarketing
- Any kind of freelance sales
- Being a personal assistant
- Aerobics instruction/personal training
- Massage therapy
- Pet care
- Catering
- Tax accounting
- Bartending
- Gardening or groundskeeping
- IT technical work or consulting
- Web designing

If you're still at a loss as to what kind of day job you should be looking for, then ask yourself these three questions.

1. "What skills do I possess that can be turned into a money-making day job with the flexibility I need?"

2. "Am I willing to learn some new skills in order to get the day job I want?"

3. "Do I want to work for myself or for someone else?"

Remember, when you're searching for the best day job you can find, be as up-front with your potential employer as possible concerning your needs as an actor. Let them know that you want the flexibility to go to auditions as well as the option of working different hours if, and when, you get acting work. If that flexibility isn't possible, then keep looking.

For Further Reading

• *How to Get a Great Job in 90 Days or Less* by Joe Carroll

• *Survival Jobs - NYC Edition: Details on How to Apply for Over 70 Companies that Hire Actors and Artists* by Michelle Dyer

• *Survival Jobs: 154 Ways To Make Money While Pursuing Your Dreams* by Deborah Jacobson

Difference #4
A Successful Actor is a great money manager.
A Starving Artist is a 24-hour ATM.

Money is only a tool. It will take you wherever you wish,
but it will not replace you as the driver.

—Ayn Rand

To build on the last chapter and its focus on finding the right day job, let me now turn to the other side of that coin, so to speak. Successful actors know that their income is only half the equation when it comes to pursuing their career goals. On the other side of the ledger are expenses that result from the lifestyle choices they make. You can earn $10,000 a month, but if your expenses run $9,995, then you've got a problem.

Too many actors allow their money to run their lives. Unfortunately, most have never been given the knowledge about how to manage it prudently or how it can end up affecting every life decision they make. All it takes is a few student loans and a couple of maxed-out credit cards to shut off the opportunities you need to advance your career.

Don't ever forget that you're the venture capitalist who's investing in this company called "Your Acting Career, Inc.," and since money for headshots, acting classes, and travel to auditions will not be falling from the trees, you need to figure out how to finance it all after you've paid your bills for the month. Not only that, but you'll need to either become well versed in the U.S. tax code, as it relates to filing your taxes as a performer, or hire someone who is. Believe it or not, the IRS has given performers a host of tax breaks and write-offs that, if taken advantage of, can mean the difference between getting a refund or writing Uncle Sam a check.

Successful actors live as simply as possible in order to have the money they need for their work. Starving artists live from paycheck to paycheck without any kind of plan for a rainy day, much less for investing in their career. Their checks are no sooner cashed than they are spent.

To help illustrate the importance of this challenge, I've reworked a little fable for you. So with apologies to Aesop, here goes:

The Grasshopper and the Ant

Once upon a time, there were two young actresses, Gretchen the Grasshopper and Agnes the Ant. They were roommates who were fresh out of acting school and just starting their careers. Both were talented and driven, but like all "newbies," they faced a dilemma. To gain experience and exposure, they needed to get acting work, but most of it paid little, if anything. So how could they solve the puzzle of doing a show and paying the bills while working fewer

TO BE OR WANNA BE

hours at, or completely leaving, their day jobs?

Gretchen was a go-getter who was charming, funny, and smart. She naturally knew how to schmooze and always made a good first impression. Unfortunately, she was also a spendthrift. It seemed she couldn't walk from the front door to her car without spending $20. Even though she made more than enough to live on from her day job, she was always asking Agnes for a loan to get her through until payday. Whenever she landed a paying gig, she would blow it all in celebrating her success.

On the other hand, Agnes had a real head for the Biz. She enjoyed the challenge of staying in touch with all of the producers, directors, and actors that she knew. Agnes understood that marketing and advertising were the key to getting people to notice and remember her. In addition, she was a thrifty gal. Early on, she had set up a special savings account—she called it her "Acting Fund"—into which she put $100 every week. From this account, she could cover the cost of working on those important, but low-paying, projects. Though she made the rounds and networked like everyone else, she was always careful to keep an eye on her money.

Now as luck would have it, they both landed leading roles in the same summer stock production of Shakespeare's Twelfth Night—Gretchen to play the role of Olivia and Agnes to play Viola. The play would be twelve weeks of work, with the theatre providing housing and the queenly sum of $100 a week. The girls were beside themselves with joy.

But suddenly, Gretchen stopped the celebration and said, "Wait a minute, I can't pay my half of the rent and the bills and feed myself on $100 a week. I spend that much on lattes, for cryin' out loud!" Agnes replied, "Well, you'll just have to dip into your savings. I mean, you do have some money put aside, don't you?" Gretchen answered wryly, "Yeah, sure, I keep it under the cushions of the sofa."

Then she perked up. "Hey Agnes," she said, "Do you think you could spot me the money to do this show? You know I always pay you back...eventually." Agnes sadly shook her head. "Though I have saved up quite a bit, it's not enough to cover both of us. Gretchen, if you'd have saved your money like I've been telling you to, you'd have enough to do this show. I'm really sorry, but I can't help you this time." So in the end, Agnes played Viola and Gretchen stayed home and watched reruns of *Dancing with the Stars*.

So remember:
A Starving Artist is a 24-hour ATM.
A Successful Actor is a great money manager.

So... Let's Get Started!

I want to show you five simple steps for getting your financial house in order and to start planning for the long-term goals you've set for your career.

1. Track every penny you spend! There's a huge difference in the way you perceive the way you spend your money and the way you actually spend it! Awareness is the key, and has been shown to be the single greatest factor in getting a handle on your finances. It doesn't matter which method you use—a cash notebook where you log every expenditure, the latest online financial tool, or some accounting software—just make it a habit! Be honest about the numbers and don't judge yourself. You're just gathering information for the next step.

2. Create a budget. After keeping track of your expenses for an entire month, use all the information you've collected to create a budget. It's one of those crucial things that separate the successful actor from the starving artist. Yes, it's boring, I'm sure you don't think you need one, and you may not even know how to make one, but that's no excuse! There are plenty of books and software programs out there that can show you how. If you can't see where you money's going, how in the world will you ever be able to direct it where you truly want it to go?

3. Spend less than you earn. Sometimes common sense is not so common, especially when it comes to money. Spending less than you earn is the holy of holies of good money management! If you don't have cash in hand to buy it...then don't! This will be easier to do once you've started tracking your expenses and have a budget up and running.

4. Get out of debt! If you're saddled with credit card or student loan debt, then make this a priority! The quick rule of thumb when dealing with multiple debts is to order your debts from the lowest to the highest balance. Decide how much money you can pay in total to all your debts. Pay the minimum payment on all your debts except the one with the lowest balance; you're going to throw every other penny at that one. Now when that debt is gone, do not alter the monthly amount used to pay your debts, but throw all you can at the debt with the next-lowest balance. It's called the "debt snowball effect," and it's a wonderful thing!

5. Now, also start your "Acting Fund." With the advent of online banking, you can now move your money around with the click of a mouse. Open a savings account and name it "My Acting Fund." Then set up a weekly debit from your checking account into this fund: $50, $100, $200...whatever you can afford. This will be the fund you'll tap into to cover expenses while you're working on that 48-hour film festival project or summer stock Shakespeare gig.

For Further Reading

• *The Money Book for the Young, Fabulous & Broke* by Suze Orman

• *The Complete Idiot's Guide to Managing Your Money, 4th Edition* by Robert Heady

• *The Laws of Money : 5 Timeless Secrets to Get Out and Stay Out of Financial Trouble* by Suze Orman

• *Financial Basics: Money-Management Guide For Students* by Susan Knox

Difference #5
A Successful Actor listens more than she talks.
A Starving Artist talks more than she listens.

So enough about me, let's talk about you. What do you think of me?

—The starving artist

at a party

DIFFERENCE #5

This may be my favorite actor joke. Every cliché has a kernel of truth buried in it somewhere, and the old saw that actors love to talk about themselves is no different. Yes, many actors, in their search for validation and acceptance, go way overboard and richly deserve the label "narcissist." But it's tricky being your own press agent and PR person, walking that fine line between self-promotion and self-obsession. Successful actors know they must promote themselves in the industry, but they also understand that in order to do so, they must create a dialogue, not act out a monologue.

That's why successful actors make it a habit to listen more than they talk: not an easy task for any actor, to be sure. And it's even more challenging to not just be a passive listener, but an active listener! Active listening means focusing entirely on what the other person is saying, and then confirming an understanding of both the content of his message and the underlying feelings, so that you can be sure your understanding is accurate.

Active listening allows successful actors to not only understand the other person, but also have their interest come across as genuine, engaged, and—dare I say it—charming. Unfortunately, starving artists not only talk more than they listen, they don't know how to listen or what to listen for. And more importantly, they fail to understand the other person's style of speaking and listening.

I want to explore this last and very important point in greater detail: that of understanding the style of how someone both speaks and listens. In this understanding lies the key to being a good listener, and by extension, a great communicator and successful actor.

Perhaps this has happened to you. You've just finished performing your scene and have gone to the director to get your notes. She says, "Wonderful. Let's do it again, but this time infuse the scene with the color blue." And you think to yourself, "Is the director crazy? What does that mean?!"

You'd think that actors, and directors for that matter, would be experts at communicating with each other, given the fact that we use language as our primary tool in telling stories. The reality is something quite different. The root cause of this problem lies in the fact that we don't understand the style of communication being used.

TO BE OR WANNA BE

Talk the Talk

Basically, there are just two styles: literal and metaphorical. Does this describe how you speak to others?

• You think of communicating as simply a way to get your ideas and information across to the other person.

• You like to keep your conversations short and to the point.

• You always try to use the right words to get across your exact meaning.

• You always focus on the details when giving instructions, because you don't want to leave anything to chance.

• If you make a request or tell someone to do something, you expect it to be carried out exactly the way you said it should be done.

If so, then you speak in a literal style.

Or is this a better description of the way you get your ideas across?

• You tend to think of a conversation as a chance to make a personal connection with the other person.

• You prefer longer conversations.

• You use comparisons and analogies to express your feelings about a given subject.

• When discussing an idea, you focus on the big picture, speaking in an abstract way.

• You count on the other person to figure out the details of what you want and how you want it done.

This is the metaphorical style.

What Did You Say?

Let's turn to the act of listening, which is the most important part of having a good conversation. When someone is speaking to you, is this how you listen to them?

• You focus on the exact meaning of their message.

• You keep asking questions until you feel you completely understand what it is they're saying.

• You work to understand the precise meanings of words because you don't like things to be vague or ill-defined.

• You tend to take all communications at their face value.

• You don't pass communications through many "filters."

Well then, you're a literal listener.

Now instead, do you listen to someone speak in this way?

• When someone is talking, you look for the overall meaning behind what they're saying.

• If you understand the general idea, you don't bother to ask any follow-up questions.

• You're more sensitive to the feelings of the speaker and the emotions behind the speech.

• You're always on the lookout for the hidden meaning behind the words.

• You pass every interaction through many "filters."

You guessed it. You're listening metaphorically.

TO BE OR WANNA BE

Clues...

I've discovered that coaching actors on the business of the Biz is an interesting combination of being a teacher, trainer, therapist, and detective. As a teacher, I'm trying to give them the ideas and logic behind why they should be doing a particular kind of marketing or choosing a certain career path. The trainer in me gives them exercises and tasks to challenge their abilities and stretch themselves both intellectually and emotionally. Listening and empathizing with their myriad fears and anxieties has taught me the value of being a lay-therapist. I had an actress say after one of our sessions, "You're the cheapest shrink I've ever had!" Finally, given that we only have about three hours together, I have to figure out what a particular actor wants and needs, and I do this by identifying his style of communication.

It starts with me reading over the pre-session worksheet I have them fill out, in which the actor tells me about his strengths and weaknesses as a performer and businessperson, his long- and short-term career goals, and how he views his "type" in the industry. As I carefully sift through all this information, trying to get a picture of this person sitting across from me, I pay close attention to the language he's used in filling out the worksheet. Is he using it in a literal sense? Is he writing in metaphor?

Then I kick off our session by asking her questions on a variety of Biz-related topics, how her personal life is going, and what she hopes to get out of our time together. Once again, I'm listening carefully for the ways in which she describes her dreams, problems, and worries. Are her sentences short and to the point, or broad in scope, with lots of metaphors thrown in?

I'm looking for clues, because I need to know how to present my ideas and advice in a way that will make sense to a client. I don't want to come off as a know-it-all, some kind of show business Yoda speaking in riddles with hidden meanings. Nor do I want to insult someone's intelligence by giving him a "See Spot run" kind of lesson. I need to allow the actor the time to answer my questions, but I also must keep the conversation focused on the important topics we need to cover by knowing when to jump in with a new idea or two. Every session should be as unique as the actor I'm working with.

Once I get a handle on an actor's style of communicating, as well as his experience and goals, I can tailor my advice to fit his needs. We'll cover one idea in depth, but skim over another concept because he already understands it, and not even bother with some other thing, as he's been doing it for years already. My challenge is to always stay one step ahead, to keep asking the right questions or offering the best answers, while still actively listening to all the client's responses.

I always know when it's been a good session; the time goes by quickly and I'm whipped. The actor looks a bit overwhelmed by all of the information and tasks I've given him, and we're both happy to have made each other's acquaintance.

Successful actors know that it's important to understand not only their own style, but also other styles of communication. If you take things literally, but the director, agent, or producer uses a metaphorical style of speaking, you can then "translate" her comments into something you can respond to. But no matter what style of speaking or listening you or the other person with whom you're dealing uses, the important thing to remember is that a successful actor chooses to be an active listener. Take a piece of advice from the actor Eli Wallach: "The big secret in acting is listening to people."

So remember:
A Starving Artist talks more than she listens.
A Successful Actor listens more than she talks.

So... Let's Get Started!

Now that you've been introduced to the literal and metaphorical style of listening and speaking, go back and really think through those questions and decide which style best describes you. Next, look at the traits for the style that isn't the one you use. Why? Because when you first strike up a conversation with someone, you can begin to see which group they fall into based on those bullet points.

Like a detective, you're learning how to draw conclusions based on the other person's subtle use of language. If they happen to listen and speak in the same style as you do, then you can trust that the two of you will most likely be on the same page. If they fall into the other group, you can then begin to translate back and forth between your style and theirs and still carry on a good conversation.

Once you've got a handle on the issue of style, you're now ready to have a go at active listening. Here are some tips on how to listen and what to listen for.

- **In general, let the other person choose the topic of conversation.**
  Yes, I know you're filled with brilliant insights on a whole host of topics, but your purpose here is to get to know the other person, not the other way around; remember the quote from the beginning of the chapter! You may throw out something general in order to break the ice, but then allow your input to be based on his responses.

- **Spend the majority of the conversation listening to the other person.**
  People in general, not just actors, love to talk about themselves. Remember the "80/20 rule": let the other person talk 80 percent of the time; you only get 20 percent! Pay attention and you'll not only figure out her style of speaking and listening, but you'll pick up a lot of details about her life. Few things are more obnoxious than constantly cutting someone off in midsentence to show off your intellect or knowledge of a specific topic.

- **Try to see things from the other person's perspective.**
  If you can relate to what he's talking about, either emotionally or intellectually, it will create empathy and even sympathy with the other person.

- **Keep an open mind and don't assume anything!**
  We all have certain biases that color our responses to topics, people, and

ideas. Try to keep these in check. You're here to get to know the other person, not to have a debate or argument with her.

- **Ask questions based on his responses.**
  You can always keep a conversation going by inquiring about some bit of information he's just given you. Just don't answer one of his questions with a question. Save that for when you're playing a psychiatrist.

- **Dig further into her chosen topic by asking her to clarify or simplify what she's said.**
  This is along the same lines as asking questions, but here you're delving deeper into a topic she's already shown interest in. Also, by reiterating the key points or important feelings that the speaker shared, you immediately demonstrate that she has your complete attention. That's always appreciated.

- **Summarize his thoughts.**
  You'll get big "first impression" points if you can recap all the different ideas that the speaker brought up on a given topic. It shows that you don't have the attention span of a flea and that you've got a brain in your head to boot!

For Further Reading
- *The Fine Art of Small Talk: How To Start a Conversation, Keep It Going, Build Networking Skills—and Leave a Positive Impression!* by Debra Fine

- *How to Talk to Anyone: 92 Little Tricks for Big Success in Relationships* by Leil Lowndes

- *Conversationally Speaking: Tested New Ways to Increase Your Personal and Social Effectiveness* by Alan Garner

Difference #6
A Successful Actor is charming.
A Starving Artist needs a lesson in etiquette.

When I heard them play, I thought their music was quite good.
But when I met them what struck me most was their charm.
They were such charming people.

—Brian Epstein, manager
of the Beatles, describing
his first meeting with the
Fab Four

DIFFERENCE #6

It seems that the notion of being charming has fallen into disfavor as of late. Too many people equate charm with being smarmy, disingenuous, or manipulative, which is unfortunate. Genuine charm is nothing like that. In fact, it can be argued that this quality of being pleasing or attractive through one's personality is one of the most important ingredients in the successful actor's career.

When it comes to interacting with people, being charming really boils down to just two things: being a good listener by understanding the art of conversation and showing a genuine interest in the person you're speaking with. The successful actor wants to be found engaging, delightful, or fascinating by others—things that require a proactive mindset. A smile, a pleasant tone of voice, and direct eye contact helps to cultivate this impression.

You've all met someone like this: a person you find appealing and who is comfortable with herself. Her charm takes the three essentials of being a successful actor—talent, type, and tenacity—and gives them that extra spark or power to attract people and situations that end up working to her benefit. At the very least, it leaves the other person with a great first impression of that actor…and we all know how important that is!

What does "being charming" mean? It means showing a genuine interest in other people's concerns and sympathy for their problems—saying what you mean and meaning what you say, sending thank-you notes, being tactful and courteous, making eye contact with people, smiling at everyone you see, and being on time.

Pearls of Wisdom

I think that becoming a person whom others find charming is, for most of us, a conscious act. Perhaps we've seen other people in our lives whom we think of as charming, or maybe we're already exhibiting some of the traits that charming people demonstrate and we have been rewarded for this behavior. Either way, it's something we decide we want to emulate. When I think about my own continuing journey toward being charming, I reflect on the two things that have had the greatest effect on me: the influence of my parents and my work in the classical theatre.

My father, James, was voted "Mr. Personality" by his graduating high school class, and before donning a fireman's rig, spent his twenties as a trav-

eling salesman working on commission. His ability to charm his clients was legendary; he was the kind of guy who could sell you your own shoes. He never missed an opportunity to send a thank-you card, always remembered everyone's name, and was sure to ask how your great aunt Beatrice's surgery went the next time he saw you. He's taught me so many things about courtesy, tact, and business etiquette over the years—all essentials of being charming.

Sandra, my mother, may just be the most enthusiastic person you'll ever meet. Couple that with her optimism and curiosity about people and life in general, and you've got the makings of a person who's never bored, always interested in what's going on, and willing to ask the questions others might think silly. I know I get these traits from her through a combination of nature and nurture.

And... have I mentioned they're both very funny people? You can't be charming without a sense of humor, and all my friends would remark, after visiting our home, how much laughter there was in my family.

It wasn't until years later, as a young actor in New York City, that I was given the chance to refine all the wonderful traits and habits I had picked up from my parents. The Pearl Theatre is an Off-Broadway classical theatre that has its own resident acting company, and in 1992 I was given the opportunity to join the group. Every member played a specific type of character found in the classical canon, and for me that role was the male juvenile: the young lover or prince who finds love for the first time or learns some important life lesson during the course of the play.

While in early rehearsals for my first show there, I was pulled aside by Sheppard Sobel, the artistic director. He could see I was struggling with my character, Leontine in The Good Natur'd Man, and he offered this advice: "Sean, relax! The audience wants to fall in love with you. All you have to do is be charming." I said, "How the hell do I act charming?!" He replied, "You don't act charming, you must simply be charming." What he meant was, by paying close attention to how my character behaved, his disposition, his manners, and his attitude, and then trusting the playwright's skill, I could then inhabit a young man who was seen by the other characters and the audience as charming. So, coming off as charming was a result of actions and choices, both onstage and off; a person (or a character) appears charming to the audience as a result of the choices he makes, not as a result of "putting on charm." It was a lesson I *never forgot, and for the next five years I had an opportunity to learn what charm was all about from some of the greatest playwrights in the Western world.*

So, am I in the running to claim the title of "Mr. Charming?" Hardly! I have days where I'm embarrassed by my decided lack of charm, grace, and etiquette, or am brought up short by how I react to life's everyday problems. It's then that I remind myself that charm is a state of being, a positive way of living my life, and something that must always be nurtured and never taken for granted. It's not something you act, it's something you are. Thanks, Shep!

Show Biz Party Mode

But starving artists seem to have never learned this essential lesson of etiquette, or else they no longer value it, as they rush to fulfill their desires. They're so preoccupied with their own problems, needs, and issues that they've forgotten how to really listen and talk to people, much less how to be sympathetic or empathetic. Every interaction is designed to get them what they want, and if the people they're conversing with are deemed unimportant or unable to fulfill the starving artists' needs, then they quickly move on. I call this the "Show Biz Party Mode" and have seen it at every networking event I've ever attended. You know what it is. The person you're conversing with is constantly looking over your shoulder trying to find someone more important to talk to, nodding at what you're saying while looking for an opening to start talking again. Author Keith Ferrazzi, in his wonderful book on networking, Never Eat Alone, calls this type "The Networking Jerk."

Another example is the person who feels he must relate to others from a place of power. Rudeness, brusqueness, and insensitivity are his only ways of interacting with someone. Of course, the ironic flipside to his behavior is being sycophantic to those whom he perceives as being more powerful than he is. The starving artist attempts to curry favor in order to gain something, all the while resenting the other person and hating himself for behaving in this most uncharming way.

So remember:
A Starving Artist needs a lesson in etiquette.
A Successful Actor is charming.

TO BE OR WANNA BE

So... Let's Get Started!

Are you charming? Here are a couple of ways to find out. Watch how you behave toward someone who's supposed to serve you or over whom you have power—the monitor at the audition, the dresser at the theatre, the production assistant on the set. Are you polite or demanding, understanding or rude?

Here's another test. How do you react when you realize that the person you're talking to can't really help you with your career? Do you go into "Show Biz Party Mode?" Well, if you're behaving like that in those situations, how do you think you're coming across to everyone else—in rehearsal, on the set, or at the audition? To quote Henry Van Dyke, "There is no personal charm so great as the charm of a cheerful temperament."

Charm 101

Here are some tips you can use to take your active listening to the next level and enter the world of charm.

While You're Listening

- Keep eye contact with the speaker, but only as much as feels appropriate; don't make her feel uncomfortable.

- Nonverbal signals such as body movements, tone of voice, eye contact, posture, and gestures can communicate important information about how the person is feeling. But beware that sometimes these signals can be misleading. It's always better to take in the whole message that his nonverbal signals are sending than to base your assessment on any one trait.

- Show her with your body language that you're paying attention by facing her, maintaining a good posture, and even leaning in slightly. Be aware of her personal space, though!

- Give him ongoing cues that you're following his idea or story. You can do this with nods, facial expressions, or murmurs such as, "Uh-huh," "So what happened next?" or "How did that make you feel?"

- One big ingredient of charm is empathy, so try putting yourself in her situation. This will help you focus on what she's saying and make your responses more insightful.

- Remember, context is important and should never be discounted; people behave differently at formal functions, informal gatherings, moments of crisis, or celebrations.

While You're Thinking

- As best you can, shut out any distractions—the newspaper you're reading, the radio or TV, other people who are not part of the conversation, and even the location where you're conversing.

- Try your best to keep your thoughts and feelings about the topic from distracting you; keep refocusing on the speaker.

- Don't think about your response while he is speaking, but keep your focus on him and what he's trying to get across. That way the conversation will flow from his thoughts and ideas, not yours.

- If you disagree with the stance the speaker has taken on a particular topic, respond in a tactful way. You're not here to debate or argue something, but rather to become acquainted with her.

- If the speaker asks you for specific advice on how to handle a given problem, then give him your best answer; otherwise, show him the courtesy of just being a sympathetic listener.

When You're Speaking

- Did you know that we can listen four times faster than we can speak? Processing information so quickly allows us to group our ideas and responses together in plenty of time, so you should allow the speaker to finish his thought before you reply. This sends the signal that you heard the entire statement, so the speaker doesn't feel the need to repeat it, and you'll know all of his points and issues.

- Ask questions to clarify what she's said, such as "Does that mean you were trying to...", and paraphrase previous statements with "So if I'm hearing you correctly..." But once again, wait until she's finished speaking to comment.

- Your tone of voice can convey a multitude of information about what you're thinking and feeling, so you should be aware of how others react to it. The more animated you make your responses, the more your interest and enthusiasm comes across as genuine.

- When a speaker's nonverbal signals are not in sync with his words, it's a sign that the person does not want to reveal or share something important. By being aware of this, you may be able to avoid making a faux pas by asking the wrong questions.

- The ability to be charming during a conversation is an acquired skill, so practice observing the speaker's verbal and nonverbal skills, as well as your own ability to focus and empathize.

For Further Reading
- *Charming Your Way to the Top* by Michael Levine

- *Miss Manners' Basic Training: Communication* by Judith Martin

- *Never Eat Alone* by Keith Ferrazzi

- *The Modern Gentleman, 2nd Edition: A Guide to Essential Manners, Savvy, and Vice* by Phineas Mollod

Difference #7
A Successful Actor builds a network.
A Starving Artist works in a vacuum.

The currency of real networking is not greed but generosity.

—Keith Ferrazzi

DIFFERENCE #7

I love that quote by Keith Ferrazzi, because it brings into stark relief one of the biggest differences between a successful actor and a starving artist. By being generous with their time, which is after all a precious commodity, successful actors create multiple opportunities for themselves; by meeting new people and strengthening established relationships, they create opportunities to further their career advancement.

"Networking" is the act of people meeting and interacting with one another for mutual professional benefit. That said, events that are set up specifically for actors to network (e.g., opening night celebrations, industry gatherings, cocktail parties) or situations that lend themselves to networking (e.g., an acting class or workshop, an audition, the holding area for background performers on a movie set) are essential to building on career successes and require a certain kind of etiquette from those present. Successful actors understand this. Starving artists, however, don't.

More often than not, they cluster together with their kindred spirits to gossip, talk shop, and commiserate about their careers. What a missed opportunity! Worse still are the starving artists who don't attend these events at all! They might as well be acting in their garage for all the good it's doing them. It's hard to believe that in this day and age of social media and our general understanding of the power of marketing, that some actors still labor under the assumption that they somehow will magically be "discovered." The only thing they're going to discover is that this show business tale is a myth.

This brings to mind that chestnut used so often in the Biz to describe a successful actor, "They were in the right place at the right time." Most people, including the starving artist, use this phrase as a stand-in for, "They were just lucky," but as another old quote says, "The harder you work, the luckier you get." There is much more going on here than luck, and it has everything to do with networking.

While there is an ingredient of luck or chance involved in an actor's success, if you look at the three elements at play in the above statement, you might see how it is possible to manipulate them in your favor. Those elements are the actor, the location, and the timing. They all have to do with networking, so let's look at each one.

TO BE OR WANNA BE

The Actor

Successful actors are willing to continually put themselves out there to meet people in the industry, even when they'd rather stay home and watch TV. Yes, it takes a great deal of time and energy to constantly seek out, prepare for, and go to these networking events; making the rounds and being charming, relaxed, and engaged can test anyone's endurance. But it must be done or your work will only exist and be recognized in a tiny sphere of the acting world. And like they say, "You're not in business to grow smaller!"

The Location

All too often, actors think they must be physically present in a given location for fortune to smile on them—such as showing up at some industry-related event. Although this is generally the case, it's not the only way to network. Through the use of postcards, email, flyers, newsletters, or just sending out a picture and resume (all elements of advertising), actors can remotely place themselves in front of the casting director, agent, or producer. In effect, they are present, but just in a different form. This is why staying in touch and networking with your contacts via advertising is so integral to creating opportunities for work to find you!

The Timing

Finally, there is the element of timing, and here is where it gets a bit tricky. Starving artists lack the tenacity to keep putting themselves in the right place again and again. Yet that is precisely what it takes in order for "the right time" to come along. You may have to audition ten times before you land a part at that certain theatre where you want to perform. Ten times, you had to work full out to put yourself in the right place until, through chance, the right time came along and the director decided to hire you.

I Schmooze, Therefore I Am

Learning how to network did not come easily to me. Like many actors, I too was the classic extrovert while onstage and introvert when offstage. I had trouble writing postcards to stay in touch or say "thank you," I would suddenly channel my inner wallflower during opening night parties, and God forbid I should actually have to ask for a business card! I just wanted to act, and this nebulous, scary thing called "networking" seemed so beyond me and my abilities that I almost gave up hope of ever understanding it. I'm sure my opening line went something like, "Hi, my name is Sean...I'm an actor...here's my card...

hire me…PLEASE!" It was excruciating.

But then, quite by accident, I learned two crucial lessons about networking that really changed my understanding of what it could do for my career and my appreciation about how it's used in the world of the Biz. The first lesson had to do with seeing the connection between networking and marketing and the second had to do with recognizing what the real goal or prize of networking is…and it's not what most actors think.

Shortly after relocating to Washington, D.C., I began meeting and working with the many actors who make this town their artistic home. During rehearsals for a production of Noises Off, playing Garry the real estate agent, I was chatting with one of the actresses in the show who seemed to really be setting the world on fire with her career. She worked all over the country and in a variety of venues. I asked her how she stayed in touch with all the people she knew in the Biz. "I send out a newsletter at Christmastime detailing most of the projects I worked on that year," she said, and she brought me a copy of one the next day. I took one look at it and my head exploded; what a great way to maintain your actor network! Then I thought, "Once a year—why not four times a year? With stories and maybe flyers or review sheets or…who knows what?"

I immediately began to experiment with this basic marketing idea, and after a few months of writing and rewriting, playing around with graphics and pictures, "The Sojourns of Sean Pratt" was born. Soon after, like clockwork, every three months I'd mail out my four-page newsletter to all the directors, producers, and casting directors I knew, recapping my recent Biz-related adventures, and thereby staying in touch with my growing network of people. When I happened to meet someone in the Biz and we exchanged business cards, I'd say, "Well, I'll stay in touch." I'd then add them to the special "Sojourns list" and they'd start receiving my quarterly news. Since it only crossed their desk four times a year, I didn't have to worry about overkill, and because the overall tone of each issue was positive, chatty, and self-deprecating, people told me they really enjoyed reading them.

I learned that gathering business cards was only the beginning. To build and maintain a network required finding creative ways to stay in touch. Then, when I met those people again, they would say things like, "Hey, your story about what happened to you on that movie set was really funny" or "That picture of you as Mister Twisty the Light Bulb Man at that energy convention was hilarious!" By the way, during the first year I starting sending out my "Sojourns," my audition calls tripled and my bookings doubled...that certainly drove home the lesson about the link between networking and marketing.

But the second, and even more important, lesson I learned had to do with discovering what the real goal and result of networking was...or you could say, the true currency of what was earned, saved, and traded. It happened quite by accident, which is usually how the best lessons are learned, and it's the main point I try to get across when teaching the concepts and steps necessary to being a good networker.

At the end of one of my "Business of the Biz" classes back in 1998, a young Hispanic actor who had attended the workshop came up and introduced himself. Michael was just starting out and eager to find on-camera work in the D.C. marketplace. I recommended that he try getting hired for the enormous number of training films that are produced here every year by the government, big corporations, and the military. He impressed me as being a real go-getter and said he would definitely follow up on my suggestions. He gave me his business card, signed up for my newsletter, and said he'd be back for more classes.

Then about two weeks later, I got a call from a video producer, whom I had worked with several times in the past, about recording some narration for an upcoming series of training films he was doing for the Army. During our conversation, he mentioned that they were still looking to cast one of the leading roles, a young private named Martinez. I said, "You know, there's an actor I met recently who might be right for that. Let me see if he's available to come to the audition." Michael was hired.

Just a few weeks later, after teaching another class, I had three actors come up and tell me how much they enjoyed the evening. "Our friend Michael told us your class was great and that we had to come, and he was right," they said. A few months after that, that same producer called me up to thank me for finding Michael, and by the way, was I available for a role in his newest video project? It was then that I realized there was a whole new dimension to networking that I had never seen before. By helping connect two people in my network—playing the role of matchmaker, if you will—I got something far more valuable than a commission or quid pro quo...I had earned their goodwill.

Goodwill, or social capital, is an intangible asset, the feeling someone has for a person or business, that comes from the positive experience they've had in dealing with them. Because I was willing to freely give of my time to help these two people solve a problem to their mutual benefit, I had been rewarded with their good opinion of my character and reputation. In this instance, it translated into more actors coming to my classes and more acting work of my own down the line. So now when I'm networking, I pay special attention to the things the other person is saying, building a catalogue of information about them that I can possibly use later. Then when I see an opportunity to help out two or more people in my network, I can connect them and earn the reward of their goodwill, bank the valuable commodity of their high opinion of me, and then spend it on the future benefits of strengthening my network and the acting projects that come my way.

So to sum up, the more you network, through advertising or being present in the flesh, and stay proactive in your day-to-day efforts, the more you generate those moments when randomness or chance will come along and create the opportunity for you to move up to the next rung on the ladder of success. Call it whatever you want—diversification, putting many irons in the fire, or just throwing mud on a wall to see what sticks. The fact is it works.

So remember:
A Starving Artist works in a vacuum.
A Successful Actor builds a network.

So... Let's Get Started!

We've all been to the actor's after-party at a cast member's house. Actors meet to network, talk shop, and either celebrate their successes or complain about their setbacks. And while these gatherings are an important way to stay in touch, blow off steam, and perhaps meet new people, they are definitely informal in nature. Unfortunately, many actors fail to realize that while their behavior at those parties can be free and easy, their conduct at professional networking events needs to be a bit more serious...and sober. Many actors end up embarrassing themselves and leaving behind a bad impression as a result. Let's look at your preparation for and arrival at the event and go over some do's and don'ts.

Ground Rules

Since these events are formal or semi-formal in nature and will have a mix of people there who work in different aspects of the industry, it is important to know the proper protocol. Take a look at these suggestions and use them when appropriate.

Before the Event

• If you can, find out who is going to be attending the event. If a certain director, playwright, producer, or agent will be there, go online and find out what they're working on at present. Or better yet, find out something about them (e.g., hobbies, mutual friends) so that you can break the ice with something other than business!

• Find out how formal the event will be and dress accordingly. It's tacky showing up under- or overdressed at a function.

• Be sure to have plenty of business cards with you, as well as some extra blank cards in case the other person forgot their business cards; the guys at Holdon Log (www.holdonlog.com) offer some as a free download! Don't worry about bringing copies of your DVD reel, audio demo, or comp card. You can send them later, and anyhow, you don't want to burden the other person with carrying these things around for the rest of the night. If a person you meet wants them, you can include these things with your follow-up letter. A quick comment here on how many items to include. Send them the things requested (e.g., your picture/resume, demo reel, comp card), and then include one or two additional pieces of advertising if you have them (a review sheet, flyer, postcard, etc.). You don't want to overload them with too many things at once. Besides, you'll want to send them updates, using these pieces of advertising, to stay in touch.

Arriving at the Event

• Be sure to arrive on time, as you don't know how long the people you want to meet with will be staying. Carefully peruse the guest list or name tags to see who will be attending and pick three or four people to meet during the event.

• Now is the time to screw your courage to the sticking place and be the one who introduces yourself first. The other person will appreciate your moxie; after all, that's why you're there in the first place! Rehearse using your full name and a short description of who you are and why you're there: "Hi Gus, I'm Sean Pratt. I'm an actor from New York City and I've just relocated here to Washington, DC. I'm trying to get a feel for what the theatre scene here is like. I understand that you're the associate artistic director at Theatre X. How has your season gone so far?"

• Now here's a tough one…especially for actors. One of the best ways to have a networking conversation is to ask questions and then actually listen to what the other person says…sound familiar? Your ratio of listening to talking should be about 80/20. If you follow that bit of advice, people will think you're a brilliant and, of course, charming conversationalist.

During the Event

• When you happen to come across a group, you should wait for a break in the conversation or for one of the members of the group to make eye contact with you. But if no one looks your way and the vibe you get is that the conversation is a bit fervent or meant to stay private, you should just say, "Excuse me," and come back later. Crashing in on a conversation is never the way to make a good first impression.

• Try not to monopolize anyone's time nor to let anyone monopolize yours. After a sensible length of time, end the chat with, "Well, it was a pleasure meeting you; have a great evening," or words to that effect.

• You may be one of the greatest whistling, tap-dancing jugglers in the country, but now is not the time to show off your skills. This is a networking event, not an audition! Don't put someone in the uncomfortable position of having to watch you perform…it's tacky, amateurish, and embarrassing.

- A quick note on business card etiquette. Don't just press your card into everyone's hands—it's obnoxious. I find the best way to get people to take your cards is to (after having a good conversation with them) ask for theirs first. Then, they usually will ask for yours—or you have at least opened the door to offer them yours.

- While alcohol is a great way to "lubricate the conversation," one too many can be a recipe for disaster. An impolitic comment, an angry tirade, or falling out of your chair because you've had one too many can definitely leave a bad impression.

When You Get Home
- Soon after the event, go through the business cards you've acquired and enter them into your database. Send your new contacts an email or letter or give them a phone call.

- If you've told someone you would do something for them, then get it done; nothing says "motivated professional" more than delivering on the promises you've made.

Finally, remember to have fun at these mixers. A relaxed and upbeat attitude is always charming and engaging; what a great venue to show people the real you.

For Further Reading
- *Professional Networking for Dummies* by Donna Fisher

- *Networking for People Who Hate Networking: A Field Guide for Introverts, the Overwhelmed, and the Underconnected* by Devora Zack

- *Self-Promotion for Introverts: The Quiet Guide to Getting Ahead* by Nancy Ancowitz

Difference #8
A Successful Actor has a personal brand.
A Starving Artist hasn't got a clue.

Regardless of age, regardless of position, regardless of the business we happen to be in, all of us need to understand the importance of branding. We are CEOs of our own companies: Me Inc. To be in business today, our most important job is to be head marketer for the brand called You.

—Tom Peters

Personal branding, a concept that has come into vogue over the last ten years, is the practice of taking people and their career or lifestyle and marketing them as a brand; they are the product and service they sell. Previously, the focus had been on self-improvement as a way of defining one's unique abilities in a given vocation, but with the advent of personal branding, the focus has shifted to self-packaging. It starts by developing the particular assets or qualities that a person has—his knowledge, expertise, business acumen, type, or appearance. Then, through marketing and advertising, he works to create a memorable impression that sets him apart from the others in his field. At its highest level, personal branding can involve endorsing a particular product or service by linking one's name to it.

Now, the majority of successful actors don't sell their own line of perfume or have a magazine named after them, but they do understand how the concept of personal branding can help them in their careers. They know that they will be typed by casting directors, agents, and directors, based on their perceived abilities and unique qualities, so they work to control this by developing, defining, and then presenting only those things they want to be known for. They carefully craft an image based on this product/service—their talent, looks, and abilities—and this, in turn, becomes their personal brand.

Not only do starving artists fail to grasp this concept, they often rebel at the mere thought of it. They feel that their talents give them the ability to play almost any role and the idea of someone typing them as one particular thing, never mind doing it themselves, is seen as anathema to being an actor. Yet what they perceive as being "pigeonholed" is really the industry assessing them and their talent in the simplest and most direct way possible. This is going to happen regardless of how they feel about typecasting, but instead of acknowledging this reality and developing a personal brand that is simple to identify and promote, they allow others to do it for them. The result is that, by their own inaction, they become just one more actor among many. This is the main reason that the old saw, "Actors are a dime a dozen," still holds true. Along with this, I feel that actors often present the most general, generic auditions in an effort not to be "typed," and thereby fail by simply not being specific enough for the director to see them in a particular role.

Why Starving Artists are a Dime a Dozen
When a product is used by many people in their daily lives, it becomes a

commodity—an article of trade or commerce, especially a product, as distinguished from a service. When something becomes a commodity (think of gasoline or milk), the main reason you buy "Brand A" over "Brand B" is price and price alone. For instance, you don't care if it comes from Shell, ExxonMobil, or the Qwiky Mart; you just want the cheapest gas possible. There are so many actors out there trying to get work that they've become a commodity as well. In general, they're not viewed as unique, or unique enough to warrant the extra things, such as more money or a better overall contract or deal, they are trying to get from the producer.

As the saying goes, "If you try to please everyone, you end up pleasing no one." Starving artists, in effect, become just a commodity because they haven't highlighted what makes them different from the other actors vying for that role—the same ones who are also marketing themselves as being able to do and be everything.

You're Special…Just Like Everybody Else

The truth is, you can't do or be everything, and it's a waste of time to try. Instead, you should focus on doing a small number of things very, very well. In business, this concept is called differentiation—the act of creating, defining, and demonstrating the distinctive features, attributes, or traits of a product or service in a positive light. Successful actors realize they must pick a handful of their unique talents and skills, along with their experience, and focus on them alone as their main selling points.

Here's an example. Let's say you have a strong desire to carve out a niche for yourself doing classical theatre. You've taken stage combat classes, performed in numerous Shakespeare plays, worked the Renaissance Festival circuit, and you can even play the lute! Okay, so why not have some promotional shots made that show you holding a sword or dressed in period clothing? Why not highlight all that training and experience on your resume by using a bold red typeface? How about including a review sheet that quotes some favorable notices you garnered while performing at some Shakespeare summer stock festival? Now, use this material when you're submitting yourself for future classical theatre work. If you don't feel comfortable putting these promotional materials with your submissions, then have them ready to hand out should the opportunity arise during the audition, and also create a place for them on your website.

Just by differentiating yourself in this simple way you send a very clear and concise message about who you are and what you can do. Now does this mean you can only present one image to the industry? No, it doesn't. But if you're going to show other facets of your abilities, they too need to have the same level of presentation to them; for instance, a different headshot, resume, or review sheet—perhaps even a different kind of media, such as an audio narration CD or TV and film reel DVD, as appropriate.

Doctors, Cops, and Priests

When I graduated from college and started my career, I had no clue about my personal brand or how to promote it. I was just another young actor showing up at auditions and hoping for the best...a dime a dozen. This was really brought home to me during one audition in particular. I was going in to read for Demetrius in A Midsummer Night's Dream. It was for a big regional theatre, and I was very excited about the possibility of working there. I had been to a number of large auditions in New York City and this one was no different; they were calling in a huge number of actors for each role. Still, having been in the city for about a year, I thought I'd seen it all...until I opened the door to the casting office.

We all know that there are thousands of actors in New York, each looking for that one big break. Now, remember when you were little and your mommy told you how special you were? How there was no one else in the world just like you? Well, when I walked into that room full of 40 other tall redheaded actors who looked just like me, all reading for the role of Demetrius, I realized that my mom had been lying!

After I got over the shock of seeing 40 doppelgangers, I found a place to sit and introduced myself to the guys seated around me. Each of them was remarking on how strange it was to see a room full of redheads, all reading for the same part. Then I noticed one guy, whom I'll call Gus, who was seated right next to the door to the audition room. As each actor exited the room, having finished his audition, Gus would pop up and pepper the actor with questions.

"What did the director ask you to do? Is she very talkative? Did she want you to be serious? Did she have you do the scene a couple of different ways? Tell me, what does she want?" he would ask.

TO BE OR WANNA BE

Finally, an actor named Mark went in. Mark was one of those guys who really knew himself, his personal brand, and what he had to offer the director for this project. He just oozed confidence, style, and focus. He always went into an audition with a plan of how to harness his brand to have the greatest effect on the director. When he came out, Gus popped up to start showering him with questions. But before Gus had a chance to get one word out, Mark turned to him and said, loudly, "Dude, the director wants ME! That's what she wants." The room erupted into gales of laughter.

The fact is, no actor can know for sure what the director is looking for at the audition; most directors don't know what they're looking for themselves! It was obvious this director wanted Demetrius to be a tall young redhead, but that was really all anyone could know going into the audition.

In an ideal world, what the director wants is the most talented actor whose essence is right for the role and fits into the overall concept of the show and with the other actors the director hires. Yet along with talent and fit, there are those intangibles, such as personality, or "vibe," that can be the tipping point as to whether or not an actor lands the part. How many times does an actor get the role simply because he made a good impression on the director, or because he went to the same school, or because he knows the same people? This all goes back to Difference #5, knowing how to talk and listen to people. There's so much more to casting than talent, look, and fit.

Your job—your challenge—is to show the director, through highlighting your personal brand (your resume, your headshot, your audition choices, your overall demeanor) that this role should be played by no one else but you! By the way, I didn't get the part, Mark did; but I did learn a valuable lesson.

In the years since, I've discovered that because of my "essence," my personal brand in the theatre is that of the "good guy" or "funny leading man." On film, it seems that I'm favored to play doctors, cops, and priests; positive, helpful, nonthreatening people. Would I like to have a shot at Macbeth or some rogue CIA agent/assassin/hunky love interest? You bet! But the reality is there are other actors whose essence and personal brand is much closer to those characters than mine will ever be.

Accepting this truth, though hard in the beginning, has helped me hone the image and perception that people in the Biz have of me and my talent. By staking out my claim to these specific kinds of characters, I've been able to build a career and branch off into other venues as well: audiobooks, commercial modeling, even teaching.

Maybe the next time around I'll be the new George Clooney. A guy can dream, can't he?

Your Essence 101

So how do you start the process of personal branding? How do you go about identifying your unique qualities and abilities, and then begin the process of refining them? It starts with understanding something I call your "essence."

The people who do the casting or hiring in our business evaluate and make casting decisions based on their observation of your essence and how they think it would fit with a particular role. Therefore, it's not only critical that you understand what your essence is, but that you learn how to manage it in order to showcase and control the message it sends out, thereby creating your personal brand. The agent's or casting director's reaction to your essence will have a direct influence on how they perceive your type and on which roles you're submitted and called in for.

1, 2, 3

There are three elements that make up your essence—your personality, your physical appearance, and your vibe. While the first two components are pretty self-explanatory, the term "vibe" needs a little clarification. Think of the energy that you bring into a room, the unspoken attitude you send out to everyone: that is your vibe. In acting terms, you would call it your subtext, so think of it as your real-life subtext. There are times we knowingly put out a certain vibe (when you're in the elevator with strangers, visiting your grandmother, dealing with the lady at the DMV) and one of the most important challenges you'll have is learning how to use your vibe, along with your personality and appearance, to create and promote your personal brand.

Take me for instance; my personality is open, friendly, and funny; my physical appearance is big, Irish, and tall; my vibe is approachable, helpful, and focused. Roll all that together and like the story title says, I end up playing doctors, cops, and priests.

But an interesting thing about these three elements is that once you are aware of them, you can, to varying degrees, alter them to suit your career aims in relation to the personal brand you've created. Lose weight, color your hair, harness the power of your personal charm…all of these things and more can be manipulated toward the positive goals you're pursuing. But be aware that there are limitations as well. If you're short, stocky, and graced with strong features, there's probably no way for you to become the willowy, sexy leading lady. Likewise, the sum total of your essence simply will not fit with certain characters no matter what you do.

Finally, once you've defined your personal brand, it must inform every Biz-related decision you make. Your headshot, your resume, your website, how you position yourself in a given market, the style and tone of your advertising—all these things are informed by the personal brand you've created. But it all starts with self-awareness and a decision to carve out a unique place in the industry. Like the Chinese proverb says, "The beginning of wisdom is to call things by their right names."

So remember:
A Starving Artist hasn't got a clue.
A Successful Actor has a personal brand.

So... Let's Get Started!

Take a few minutes and see if you can come up with words or descriptive phrases which capture your essence. Take a piece of paper and write down five to ten things that describe your personality, your physical appearance, and your vibe. If you want to go a step further, ask ten to twenty people who know you in different contexts (family, work, friends, etc.) the following three questions:

1. How would you describe my physical appearance?
2. How would you describe my personality?
3. What kind of "vibe" do I give out on any given day?

Hopefully you'll get some honest and insightful answers to these questions. The idea is to take their feedback and use it to become more aware of your essence.

Next, list the kinds of roles you typically get called in for or have played recently. Which part of your essence would you say was most responsible for you getting those auditions or parts? Or was it a combination of them? Do you see a connection between how the essences of these characters fit with your essence? You may be surprised at what you discover. A caveat to young actors: The roles you get in high school or college should not define how you see/brand yourself. These castings happen in a virtual vacuum—particularly when it comes to age.

For Further Reading
• *It's a Branded World* by Michael Levine

• *The Personality Code* by Travis Bradberry

Difference #9
A Successful Actor behaves like a CEO.
A Starving Artist acts like a temp.

The ancients knew very well that the only way to understand events was to cause them.

—Nassim Nicholas Taleb

Successful actors know that they are a company, both literally and figuratively. Literally, like a company, they choose which industry and marketplace to work in, are always searching for new customers for their products and services, want their business to grow every year, and compete against other companies for market share. Figuratively, they make up all the employees of their company: the secretary, the marketing director, the mailroom clerk, the head of advertising, and most importantly, the CEO!

While starving artists allow their careers to drift aimlessly from job to job, like a temp worker with no charted path for their endeavors, successful actors approach their career choices with great care and attention. They think like a CEO in that they are constantly creating and then carrying out strategies for their "company." There are four basic jobs that any CEO must do in order to be truly effective. Let's look at each one and see why they're so important.

The Board of Directors

To begin with, the CEO must recruit and work with a board of directors. In the business world, this board gives the CEO advice on the big issues facing the company, uses their own connections to help the CEO partner up with other people or companies for their mutual benefit, has a hand in developing new strategies for growing the company, and ultimately holds the CEO accountable for his or her actions. Successful actors gather their own personal "board of directors," or team of advisors and mentors, if you want to think of them that way, who have an interest in that actor's success. This is not to be confused with having an accountant, lawyer, or financial advisor, although you may need them also. Those people are being hired for their services, and that's a different relationship altogether.

No, this particular board of directors believes that helping this actor become more successful is important and are willing to volunteer their time and assistance. So who's on this board? Well, anyone connected with our industry would be an obvious choice (college professors, directors, and producers you may know; successful actors you've worked with; stage managers, agents, and so forth), but the successful actor is always on the lookout for some successful entrepreneur, artist, or simply a "wise old soul" to ask as well.

R & D

Next, the CEO decides where and how much money the company will invest in research and development (R&D). Like a good company, successful actors know that they must constantly improve their product/service in order to stay competitive and survive. Ultimately, someone is paying you in exchange for something of value, and if you don't improve what you have to offer, then when the market begins to change and want something else, you won't be able to stay current.

Most companies spend about 5 percent of their revenues on R&D. Successful actors wisely choose which things will give them the most return on their investment (ROI). Think about it: if you make $25,000 a year, you should be spending $1,250 on your actor R&D. However, starving artists look at that expense and think it's too much to spend, not worth the expense, or that their skills are just fine. Which attitude do you think will pay off in the end?

There's an App for That!

Third, the CEO works tirelessly to market the company's "solutions" (which is business-speak for their product or service). When you go to an audition, you are being seen as a possible solution to the director's problem of casting the right actor for that role. Successful actors realize that the more aggressively they market themselves in the industry as a possible solution for a role or project, the better their chances of getting an audition. They define their personal brand and then carefully project that image out to the people in the Biz. It's called marketing, advertising, and networking, and no actor succeeds without it.

Starving artists don't even think in these terms, and they allow others to type them. Or worse, they thoughtlessly use the Internet or social media to put out information, photos, or comments that are less than flattering. Google, Facebook, and Twitter remember everything…you should never forget that! Even if actors grumble about typing, it's much more empowering to type oneself or determine one's own essence for marketing purposes than to be default-typed by others. And since you can tweak the three elements of your essence, or brand, to a certain degree, you can work to change how you are viewed in the industry, thereby changing the categories that make up your type. Looking for a challenge? Now that's a challenge worth pursuing!

If You Can Make It There, You Can Make It Anywhere

Finally, successful actors, working as the CEO of their company, think with a global perspective. They are not limited by the market (theatre, film, voiceovers) or the marketplace (New York, Los Angeles, Washington, D.C.) they work in. They are willing to travel, relocate, or even take the plunge into a new kind of performance work if they see an opportunity for growth or advancement. Starving artists don't realize that they must be willing to live, work, learn, and develop a wide range of options for their talents to flourish.

Sean Pratt, Inc.

I didn't become a CEO until a series of life-changing events forced me to truly take charge of my career. As the saying goes, every crisis holds the seeds of opportunity, and I was fortunate enough to see the potential for not only reshaping my career, but fundamentally transforming the way I thought of and approached decisions concerning it. I had just moved to Washington, D.C., after a successful seven-year stretch of working in New York, to start my life and career over with my then-girlfriend and now-wife, Shannon Parks.

To help in the transition to this new town, I had lined up parts in three plays—what I thought would be nine months of acting work—at one of the biggest theatres in town. Having worked there previously, given a great audition for the roles, and after meeting with the artistic director, I knew everything was going to work out fine. My master plan was to hit the ground running, or should I say rehearsing, and then spend the next several months getting a feel for Washington and what it could offer me. But soon after my arrival, I gave the theatre's casting office a phone call to check in and I heard the phrase every actor dreads, "We've decided to go in another direction with these roles." (Insert sound of my jaw hitting the floor.)

The very next day, I called my New York agent to figure out what I should do now, and was told the next-worst thing an actor could ever hear, "Sean, we're reorganizing the agency and dropping all of our out-of-town actors...and that includes you." (Insert sound of me hitting the floor.)

As I lay there, curled up in the fetal position, desperately wanting to wake up from this nightmare, I heard the words of my father come back to me once again: "What's your Plan B, Sean?" Not only was there no Plan B, but by losing my New York agent, my whole world had been turned upside down. Like so many actors, I had come to rely on him to make all the big decisions for me, guide my career, and do all the heavy lifting in regard to marketing me in the industry. It was as if, after all those years of hard work, I was right back where

TO BE OR WANNA BE

I started. Yet I soon discovered that sometimes starting from scratch can be the most liberating and invigorating thing that can ever happen to you.

The first thing I did, once I literally picked myself up off the floor, was to grab my paintbrush and hammer and scare up some work as a handyman; the bills still have to get paid, you know? Next, I started contacting every person I thought could help me brainstorm some new ideas, give me some perspective on my situation, and offer some advice and encouragement. They were a collection of friends, colleagues, and acquaintances from across the country that I had known for some time and were some of my biggest supporters. This group eventually became my own personal board of directors, who would motivate and challenge me to restart my career.

Soon after that, I began investing my time in researching this new marketplace and finding out who the real players were, networking with the actors I met, and discovering just how different D.C. is from New York. Then I started to develop a plan to capitalize on all this information, got new pictures, and reworked my resume to fit this unique town—and in the process changed the look and feel of what the company called Sean Pratt, Inc. sold.

Next, realizing that I was now responsible for marketing myself to all these new casting directors, theatres, producers, and directors, I taught myself the ins and outs of advertising, graphic design, business etiquette, and so much more. I came to understand that I could create my own personal brand by controlling the information I sent out and the impressions I made on people, and that this could further my career goals. And thanks to my years of work in New York, I had developed the confidence to promote myself, or as they say, "tirelessly push my company's solutions," to the powers that be.

Finally, I began to look for other markets besides theatre in which to find work, and was surprised to discover many options available to me. Narrating audiobooks, commercial modeling, on-camera hosting for training videos, small parts in the TV and film projects that were being produced in the area—all these opportunities and more were out there for the taking, and not just in D.C., either. By traveling up to Philadelphia and Baltimore and down to Richmond and Wilmington, the number of job opportunities and venues grew exponentially. Soon I was putting down my hammer, and for the first time in my career, was working full-time as an actor. It was simply amazing.

DIFFERENCE #9

In the end, successful actors, like good CEOs with their companies, understand that their overall task is to be mindful of their career; build a group of mentors whom they ask for help; wisely choose how they invest their time and money; carefully decide what image they want to project; and keep a vigilant eye on how they view their career in relation to existing opportunities.

So remember:
A Starving Artist acts like a temp.
A Successful Actor behaves like a CEO.

TO BE OR WANNA BE

So... Let's Get Started!

Job #1—Building Your Personal Board of Directors

When you decide that someone would be a great member of your board, reach out to him with a proposal. Let him know how much you've admired his previous advice and help in the past, or that because of his particular business or life experience, he could offer a great deal of insight into the Biz. Tell him that you would like to talk or meet with him on an occasional basis...say once every three to four months via phone or email, or perhaps in person.

Then you can work with him to brainstorm ideas for your career, create challenges for you to overcome, keep you focused on your goals, or talk about the obstacles you're encountering and how to deal with them. For the cost of lunch or drinks, you will come away with more advice and ideas than you could ever afford to buy.

Job #2—Research and Development

How much do you spend on your voice, acting, or dance classes? Are you buying time to work with a business coach or getting your certification as an actor combatant? What about those music lessons and Shakespeare workshops? This is the "actor R&D" I was talking about, and your level of interest and investment into these areas will be the difference between becoming a more successful actor, or revisiting the world of the starving artist. Deciding what to focus on is a matter of first setting specific goals for the year ahead.

To begin with, choose five, and only five, career-related goals to accomplish for the coming 12 months. Five seems to be about the right number—not too many, not too few. Now, "career-related" can mean many different things. Is this the year you want to quit smoking? Get back in shape? Find a new day job that has more flexibility? These goals aren't directly related to your career, per se, but they will definitely have an effect on it. Of course, you'll want to pick straightforward goals, too. You could get certified as an actor combatant, earn more EMC points for your Equity card, or work at breaking into audiobook narration. Whatever you decide, just pick five. These will make up your actor research and development.

For example, let's say you're moving to a new town, Washington D.C., and you pick these five goals:

- Find acting work at theatres in the D.C./Baltimore area.
- Find a day job in D.C.
- Research all agents, casting offices, etc. in the D.C./Baltimore area.
- Get a car!
- Lose ten pounds.

Next, take each goal and break it down into smaller sub-goals. For example:

1. Find acting work at theatres in the D.C./Baltimore area.
   - Develop a list of theatres I'm interested in working with.
   - Start networking with D.C. actors.
   - Decide what styles of theatre I'm interested in.
   - Research any general theatre auditions.
   - Begin working on new audition material.

Then take each one of these sub-goals and break them down into smaller and smaller pieces.

Develop a list of possible theatres.
1. Professional Equity houses.
2. All theatres doing classical and known works. No musicals or touring shows!
3. D.C. and Baltimore area only!
4. Find out which theatres have good reputations and which to stay away from.
5. Research any resident acting companies.

Putting Your Plans into Action

Eventually, you'll get down to tasks that can be accomplished on a daily basis. Plan ahead and write out these specific tasks on a big wall calendar. This will allow you to bounce back and forth between your various goals. So when you wake up on any given morning and ask yourself, "What can I do today that will move my career forward?", you can answer, "Oh, today I'll continue my research into theatres that have resident acting companies, I'll go to the gym, and I'll call the box office of the Folger Theatre and get on their mailing list."

Now even if you only manage to do one of these tasks, know that at the end of the day you have moved your career forward one more step. That one step, added to all the others, will separate you from 99 percent of the people out there who want to be actors. One phone call, one email, or one hour spent working on a monologue every day, is all it takes to gather the momentum that will propel you forward.

The Year in Review

On a quarterly basis, pick some morning to sit down and look over your list of goals to see how much progress you're making. Then, at the end of 12 months, go through the list one more time. Maybe you've completed goals #1 and #4, are coming close to completing goals #2 and #5, and goal #3...well, you just couldn't keep that one on track, but there's always next year. Now ask yourself, "Am I successful? Have I moved forward in my career? Was all the effort and hardship worthwhile and am I moving towards the goals I set?" You'll know the answer.

Job #3 — Reach Out and Touch Someone

Marketing your company's "solution" to directors, agents, and other casting people is difficult, to say the least. Every day they are bombarded by actors trying to sell their solutions too. Did you know that we now receive more information in one day than our great-grandparents did in a month? To cope with this tsunami of data, our brains have learned to filter out the majority of this information; only paying attention to those things which are repeatedly or ingeniously brought to our attention. This is exactly what happens for the casting director or agent as they cope with a never-ending stream of pictures and resumes. To help solve this problem, the marketing world came up with "the five-touch rule."

The Five-Touch Rule

The five-touch rule is a marketing concept meaning that the consumer must be "touched" through advertising about a product/service at least five times before they can begin to recognize and recall it.

In its simplest form, you "touch" the director or agent every time they receive your picture/resume. But though this concept is easy to understand, it needs an imaginative touch in order to have a real effect. You don't want to just send them your headshot five times and hope for the best!

The Nuts and Bolts

Rule number one of any marketing campaign is that the consumer must see the product in every advertisement so they can link it to the service it provides. For you, this translates into always putting your picture on anything you send out. The only exception would be your voice-over CD, because you want them to cast you for your voice and not your look. So here are some examples of how to use your advertising materials to touch someone in the Biz.

• Every month or two, use your photo postcards to keep them up to date with what you're doing. Even if you're not working, you can still tell them about the classes you're taking, who was casting or directing the project you were called back for, or those new pictures you're getting ready to shoot.

• Create a review sheet—a collection of reviews, plus images of the show poster or pictures—from the show you're currently in, which highlight your work.

• Craft letterhead and "thank you" notes with your picture on them to be used in all correspondence.

• If you have a film reel, be sure to incorporate your picture and resume into the packaging.

Reach Out and Really Touch Someone

After you've started touching them through these basic methods, it's time to get a little more creative...and personal. Try to find different ways of either putting yourself in their presence or participating in some event where you will have a shared experience; after all, you're much more engaging in person. As a follow-up touch to these ventures, be sure to write to the appropriate people telling them how much you enjoyed the experience. Here are some examples:

• Pick a theatre you're interested in and usher at a show. Better yet, snag a ticket for opening night and introduce yourself to the director at the party afterward.

• Find out if a theatre needs volunteers to help strike a set. It's amazing what you can learn about an organization this way.

• Search out any industry-related events happening in your area. Think award ceremonies, theatre conferences, panel discussions, and the like.

• If a particular agent or casting director is teaching a class, then save up your pennies and attend…this is called "pay to play."

Remember that five touches are only the beginning. These are part of an ongoing campaign to gain and maintain the attention of the various people in the Biz who are the gatekeepers to your success.

Job #4—Be the Master of Your Domain

The impetus for starting this whole process is the idea that the possibility exists for you to grow your business: to move into a new geographical marketplace, a new product market, or to increase your market share in a particular area. You can draw this conclusion from one of two observations.

• You recognize the opportunity to break into a new marketplace or market. "If I'm willing to travel, I might be able to get more work in the Philadelphia marketplace" or "Hey, I'm really interested in breaking into the market of audiobook narration!"

• You see the potential to expand your career opportunities in a market you're already working in. "I want to do more audio narration projects here in Los Angeles" or "This kind of theatre work is great, but I want to do more projects of a higher quality at better venues."

Time to Dig Deeper

Next, you ask yourself these questions:

• What is required of me to compete in this marketplace or market? Is travel a factor? How about being union or non-union? If you want to work in commercial modeling, will you have to lose 20 pounds?

• What kind of training might be necessary to meet these requirements, and how much will that cost? If you want to do summer stock musicals, then maybe it's time to find a voice coach. What will be the ongoing cost of that?

• How long will it take before I can start marketing myself in this new market? One class in stage combat does not make you a stuntman. And you don't want to put down on your resume that you can swing dance until you've had enough training to really show it off.

• What kind of advertising materials will I need and how much will they cost? Want to break into commercial modeling? Then you're going to need a comp card. You'll have to investigate how you create one, the cost of shooting the pictures, and what the price of reproductions will be.

• How much work and money do I think I can earn? You need to explore and then decide if the return on the investment of your time and money is really worth the effort of working in that marketplace or market.

• Are there any other issues associated with pursuing this goal? You may want to go on that nine-month tour, but how will that affect your partner or family? If you want to go back to school for your MFA, will you be taking yourself out of the theatre or film market at just the moment when you could really make some headway in your career?

OK, you're the CEO and it's time to earn your keep! Answering all these questions will help you decide if it's worth pursuing this new opportunity or something else, instead. But either way, be brave, think big, and bang your own drum!

For Further Reading
• *The CEO of YOU* by Marsha Petrie Sue

• *Outliers—The Story of Success* by Malcolm Gladwell

Difference #10
A Successful Actor Thinks Like
Leonardo da Vinci.
A Starving Artist Thinks Like
Homer Simpson.

Blinding ignorance does mislead us. O! Wretched mortals, open your eyes!
—Leonardo da Vinci

How is education supposed to make me feel smarter? Besides, every time I learn something new, it pushes some old stuff out of my brain. Remember when I took that home winemaking course, and I forgot how to drive?
—Homer Simpson

Acting, when done right, is a joyful but draining experience; every scene should "cost" you something both physically and emotionally. So when we're not working, it's important to fill that time with endeavors that enliven and enrich us, not to simply lie fallow. Successful actors understand this and are constantly seeking out new and varied experiences that will not only enhance their work, but also make them a more complete human being.

The starving artist's behavior is the antithesis of this. All too often, they show a decided lack of interest in cultivating their intellect and expanding their knowledge of the world around them. If it's not directly connected to getting them a job or some other Biz-related activity, then they're simply not interested. Ironically, the times when an actor is working the most can be the least productive in regard to this quest; with our focus solely on getting the show up or the film shot, our view is necessarily narrowed. The result, though, is a lack of both depth and breadth in one's intellect and life experiences.

So how do you go about enhancing and expanding your mind and character as well as continuing the journey toward becoming the artist you want to be? Well, when in doubt, you should always seek out a great role model or mentor. One of the best books on self-improvement you will ever read is How to Think like Leonardo da Vinci by Michael Gelb. Not only does he reveal the essence of what made Leonardo a genius, he also showcases the methods that da Vinci used to keep improving on his already substantial gifts.

In his book, Gelb outlines seven important areas Leonardo used to cultivate his genius, along with the activities he did to enhance each area.

1. Curiosità (Curiosity): An insatiably curious approach to life and the pursuit of lifelong learning.
   Curiosity is the spark that ignites an artist's creative efforts. As actors, we should always be asking those six magical questions when working on a project, "Who, What, When, Where, How, and Why;" da Vinci asked them about everything.

2. Dimostrazione (Demonstration): A commitment to test knowledge through experience and a willingness to learn from mistakes.
   Leonardo knew that the only way to really test knowledge was in the act of doing. We should do the same. This allows us to transcend our known beliefs

and to grow beyond what we were yesterday, which is the only path that leads to discovering your true voice as an artist.

3. **Sensazione (Sensation): The continual refinement of the senses as the means to enlivening one's experience.**

Whether it was the food he ate, the music he listened to, or the places he went, Leonardo chose them carefully in order to rejuvenate and refine his senses. He knew that this awareness gave him new insights into his work.

4. **Sfumato (Ambiguity): A willingness to embrace paradox and uncertainty.**

Though this term is commonly used in art to describe the blurring of the sharp outlines in a painting by blending one tone into another, it has also acquired this other meaning as well. Interestingly, people who have a healthy sense of humor as well as a good connection to their inner feelings, like Leonardo, can both handle the stress that sfumato brings and dissipate it by identifying the true nature of that stress.

5. **Arte/Scienza (Art and Science): The development of the balance between science and art, logic and imagination; we now refer to this as "whole-brain" thinking.**

We've all bought into this idea that we're either a left-brained (science-oriented) or right-brained (art-oriented) person, and while it's true that one of the two tends to predominate, there's no reason why we shouldn't try and bring them into balance...like Leonardo did.

6. **Corporalitá (Health and Well-being): The cultivation of ambidexterity, fitness, and poise.**

Leonardo understood the importance of what we now call the "mind/body connection": how our physical state affects our attitude and how our attitudes affect our physical well-being. He said that we must take responsibility for our own health, both physical and mental. So he pursued a physical regimen that included aerobic and strength training, with an emphasis on flexibility. Though he didn't know it at the time, he borrowed a page from Eastern thought and advocated the idea of being fully present in all our daily activities. Buddhists call it "mindfulness." Finally, he espoused the notion that being able to use both hands equally well created a greater sense of balance in the mind and body. Those of you who play the piano know exactly what he meant.

7. **Connessione (Connection): A recognition of and appreciation for the interconnectedness of all things and phenomena; what we in the 21st century call "systems thinking."**

Human beings are hardwired to seek out patterns in the things we see and experience, as well as a desire to connect with those things that we perceive to be good—health, love, and the divine. But beyond that, da Vinci sought to find connections among the physical, the emotional, and the intellectual. The result of making such connections is a brand new way of seeing or creating, yet, ironically, by using the same old elements of the things we saw and experienced before.

Food for the Soul

I finally met Leonardo da Vinci when I was 32. Don't get me wrong, I had heard of him long before we met; I had seen some of his paintings and sketches, read about some of his more famous inventions and ideas, watched a boring BBC documentary about his life, even heard that song he wrote for Nat King Cole. But it wasn't until 1998 that we had a chance to really sit down and chew the fat, artistically speaking.

My wife Shannon had arranged this little meeting by giving me copy of Michael Gelb's How to Think Like Leonardo da Vinci as a present. "I saw it in the bookstore and thought you'd like it. You can read it when you're working on set," was what she said. Even back then, she knew me well enough to know that my Type-A personality, combined with my science/history/logic geekiness, would jump at the chance to read something like this. Yet its title did give me pause. I mean, how could I, a guy from Oklahoma one generation off the farm, hope to emulate the thinking of the world's most famous Renaissance man?

But Gelb, after introducing Leonardo and I, and giving me a thoroughly entertaining account of Leonardo's life and works, patiently outlined the seven areas where da Vinci applied his genius, along with the methods he used to enhance his senses, the results that came from them, and how I could replicate them. This, to quote Shakespeare, totally rocked! If there's one thing that gives me a sense of security and confidence, it's structure, methods, and plans. Gelb and Leo—his friends call him Leo, you know—more than delivered on their promise.

Now, I want to make it clear that I already had some of the same impulses to pursue the people, places, situations, and activities that Gelb elaborates on, but they were hit and miss at best. So by showing me how to go about it in a systematic fashion, as well as tying it back to da Vinci and his life and works, the book helped me achieve a fuller and richer experience in my efforts at enhancing my five senses. Since then, I have read and reread this book, reacquainting myself with the various exercises, reminding myself to pursue one or more of the seven areas I may have neglected recently, and building on the previous experiences I've had from doing all things da Vinci. I've assigned this book to many of the students for whom I've done career coaching and been gratified to see them achieve the same kind of results I have. I tell every artist I meet to give a read and see if it doesn't open up new vistas of experience for them. I'm even considering making a bunch of those neon-colored wristbands with "WWLD?" on them…."What Would Leonardo Do?"

For the actors who wish to grow beyond their present mind-set and abilities, I can think of no better example than Leonardo, and no more enjoyable method for doing so than Michael Gelb's book.

So remember:
A Starving Artist Thinks Like Homer Simpson.
A Successful Actor Thinks Like Leonardo da Vinci.

So... Let's Get Started!

I know that some of these concepts may seem a bit esoteric or "artsy-fartsy," but if you let yourself explore them one at a time and allow these ideas and actions to become a habit, you'll be giving yourself the opportunity to grow beyond the old you and into a new...dare I say, Renaissance...man or woman. So here are some basic applications, methods, or situations that I used when I first began to put Leonardo's ideas, and Gelb's exercises, to use. I hope they enliven your senses as much as they have mine.

Curiosità (Curiosity): An insatiably curious approach to life and the pursuit of lifelong learning.

Gelb identifies a process that Leonardo created to allow him to jump-start his curiosity when he was stymied with his work. These three specific methods also helped him approach his efforts with a certain level of objectivity. The structure is important here, for as Stanislavsky says, "Through repetition comes freedom"; meaning, if you approach your work systematically, it will ultimately allow you a thorough understanding of what you want to achieve and a means to try all the options available.

• Changing the perspective with which you view your work. Videotape your audition monologues and pretend to be watching some other actor perform. What habits or problems do you see? Now imagine you're an acting coach. What advice would you give to that actor in order to refine the performance? By the way, Leonardo used to look at his paintings in the reflection of a mirror in order to see them differently.

• Take regular breaks when working on your art in order to see it with new eyes. No scene, dance, or sword fight was ever fully created in one attempt. There comes a point when the creative juices run dry and need to be replenished. When da Vinci hit a wall with his work, he would walk away from it and spend time out in the world refreshing himself with the familiar and collecting new experiences that enlivened him. Then, when he returned to his studio, he had both the energy and the desire to engage with his art again.

• Observe and evaluate your current projects and your career from a great distance. This means pulling back and separating yourself from your work—physically, mentally, and emotionally. Take time away from your work—think mini-vacation—and create a space, both real and imaginary, for you to become as emotionally detached as possible while reviewing your past accomplishments and future challenges. From atop this cloud, you will begin to have new insights on the arc of your life and career, as well as this particular project's place in it. By increasing the timeline or scale by which you're viewing events, some mountains will become molehills and you'll start to see the forest in spite of the trees.

Dimostrazione (Demonstration): A commitment to test knowledge through experience and a willingness to learn from mistakes.

It was this concept that inspired me to create my "Plan, Act, Reflect" method, which I detail in Difference #2. Here's a quick overview:

• Plan—Before the project begins, set very clear goals for yourself, create a yardstick to measure your success or growth, and fashion a detailed plan of action.

• Act—When rehearsing, monitor what's happening to you; you're setting up a feedback loop. Specificity is important. The more detailed the observations you make, the better you can adjust the direction of your performance in relation to your goal.

• Reflect—While working, review your notes, evaluate what's working and what isn't, and continue to challenge yourself by creating a new plan to deal with any problems that come up. Finally, when the project is over, go over the whole experience in relation to how you dealt with your challenges. Where did you succeed? What could you have done differently? What were the unique circumstances of this project that either helped you or created roadblocks? And last, how will you use this experience to make your next performance even better?

Sensazione (Sensation): The continual refinement of the senses as the means to enliven one's experience.

Unfortunately for us, this effort is made all the more difficult by the fact that we are bombarded with so much information that we can literally experience sensory overload, resulting in a deadening of all our senses. But you must make the effort to find ways to create and maintain an environment that will engage and enliven your senses, too. If it worked for Leonardo, it'll work for you. Here are some suggestions you might try in order to enhance your perceptions of the world around you.

- Enroll in a class that will engage an often neglected part of your talents or skills as an actor—dancing, singing, stage combat, or improvisation.

- Practice the Buddhist method of "mindfulness." This practice involves becoming fully aware of what you are doing in the present moment, without judging it as good or bad, and not dwelling on the past or projecting forward into the future. Usually it takes the form of focusing on what your senses are experiencing—your breathing, your walking, the sounds you're hearing, and so on.

- Sign up for a course or a group that will give you a greater appreciation of some task, job, or vocation that either interests you or will allow you to deepen your knowledge of it. A cooking class, a literary society, horseback riding lessons, an art appreciation class, a gardening club, or a cycling group...all these will expose you to new and varied experiences.

Sfumato (Ambiguity): A willingness to embrace paradox and uncertainty.
The realization that a true "black or white" understanding of situations or decisions does not exist in our world is to embrace sfumato. Of course, we all like things to be "either/or" and to go according to plan—and when they aren't or they don't, when uncertainty and ambiguity are present, it creates a great deal of anxiety for us. Just think how you feel when a show closes and you have no new project to start on; will you ever work again? Here are some tips on how to deal with ambiguity in your acting career.

- Prioritize your five acting goals (we covered this in the R&D section from Difference #9) and then pick one or two that stand the best chance of immediate success. Accomplishing something early on will give you confidence and help build momentum for going after the tougher goals on your list. Be careful, though, about being distracted or adding too much to your "to do" list, as this is a quick way to become overwhelmed and then ambivalent about your prospects for success.

- Realize that if you wait for the perfect time to come along, you will be missing a window of opportunity for the possibility of success. Be willing to live with a margin of error and spring into action when things are "as good as they're going to get."

- One of the most ambiguous situations actors find themselves in is the audition. If you learn which aspects of the audition you control, and then focus on mastering those things, you'll be better able to handle the feelings of anxiety that this ambiguity can cause.

Arte/Scienza (Art and Science): The development of the balance between science and art, logic and imagination; we now refer to this as "whole-brain" thinking.

One of the main methods Leonardo used to both achieve this balance and generate new ideas was a technique we now refer to as "mind mapping." This brilliant exercise allows you to put your ideas down on paper in a graphic rather than a linear way; since you naturally generate ideas before you organize them, mind mapping lets you follow a particular train of thought for as long as you want to, then lets you switch and follow another one. You'll discover that this method of brainstorming uses your imagination and creative talents as well as your logic and organizational skills. There's even mind mapping software available for you high-tech types! Though you should refer to Gelb's book for a complete explanation of this method, here are some things to remember when you try it out:

- Always start at the center of the page with the title or image of the subject or idea you're going to be brainstorming on. From this center, you'll branch off into various directions as ideas and images come to you. If you'd like to see what a mind map looks like, simply search the phrase online; there are plenty of examples.

- Use colored pencils or markers, symbols, icons, or upper- and lowercase words for emphasis and easy-to-follow connection lines when creating your map.

- Allow yourself to bounce back and forth between ideas as you work, but keep the words and phrases on the page concise. Think of them as bullet points that represent larger and more complex ideas.

Corporalitá (Health and Well-Being): The cultivation of ambidexterity, fitness, and poise.

If you haven't heard it from an acting teacher yet, let me be the first to tell you, "You are your instrument and you must keep it in as fine a shape as possible!"

Rehearsing for a play like Hamlet is equivalent to training to run a marathon, while shooting scene after scene on a movie is like running sprints all day long. Singing and dancing in a play that performs eight times a week, rehearsing and performing two different summer-stock shows simultaneously, or having the strength and stamina to do a stunt take after take...only the actor who takes her physical well-being seriously, maintains the proper diet, and gets lots of sleep and regular exercise will be able to meet these challenges and not collapse from exhaustion or end up getting hurt.

Simply put, you should pursue the goal of staying fit and not doing harmful things to your body. It means eating right, not drinking too much, and putting down the cigarettes! Our line of work requires a tremendous amount of energy and stamina, as well as physical flexibility and mental acuity. How in the world will you be able to meet your own (as well as the director's) expectations for your work if you're hung over, out of shape, or not thinking clearly?

Not only will staying fit allow you to fully meet the requirements of a project, but you'll also reap the positive benefits of all the anxiety that gets released. Becoming proactive about dealing with the stresses of being an artist—and for that matter, being proactive in general—is an essential component of dealing with your career as a professional. Blowing off steam in a positive way is critical for maintaining your mental health. On a more serious note, dealing with chronic depression or a host of other issues that can affect your outlook is no joke. They will have a direct bearing on your ability to meet the many demands of your acting career, and if you need medical or therapeutic assistance for such issues, make sure to get it.

Connessione (Connection): A recognition of and appreciation for the interconnectedness of all things and phenomena; what we in the 21st century call "systems thinking."

Systems thinking is the practice of understanding how things, people, ideas, actions, and so forth affect each other within their own particular world or organization. When problem solving, we use systems thinking to look at how these many different parts are causing a problem and also how they can be used to contribute to the solution. Here are a few examples of how you might use this idea in your work.

- Think about the moment when your insight into a character is sparked by your manipulation of colors, words, your costume, and input from the director and the other actors. By using these different but interconnected sources of input, you begin to create depth to your character as well as sharpen the edges of the character's personality.

- You keep finding yourself catching the nasty cold that always seems to make the rounds in the cast during a show. By examining how clean your dressing room is, the people whom you come in contact with who are always sick, the measures you all are taking to cut down on spreading germs, and your own state of health and wellness, you can begin to lower the odds of you sneezing and coughing your way through another play.

- If you work in a smaller marketplace, then you should task yourself with finding out who the real players are in your city, how and if they know each other, and what actions you might take to create opportunities to advance your career with them. You must explore your universe; know all the planets, their orbits, and how they push and pull one another, along with the comets and shooting stars, before you can successfully make use of all the possibilities they present.

Finally, there's one overarching concept of da Vinci's that Gelb gives us: synesthesia, or the merging of all the senses. In essence, you're taking the seven previous concepts, and their ability to enliven your five senses, and applying them in new and different ways. What would your character sound like if she were a song? What color is this dance? How would you paint your swordfight? Leonardo developed this technique to visualize his ultimate goal for a given project and then use it as a roadmap to achieving it.

For Further Reading
- *How to Think Like Leonardo da Vinci* by Michael Gelb

- *A Whole New Mind* by Daniel Pink

Epilogue

EPILOGUE

So there you have it: the ten essential differences between a successful actor and a starving artist. I hope that your brain is abuzz with plans to put these concepts and ideas to use. Remember, I said at the beginning, this is a book you act on and not one you just read once and add to your bookshelf. I'll even go further, and say that if you're truly committed to becoming a successful actor, it's a book you live...24/7. Yes, I know that sounds a bit over the top, but I wouldn't make that claim if I hadn't been doing it myself for the last 25 years.

Every day when I get up, I ask myself, "What can I do today that will move my career forward?" and I base my answer on these ten differences. Do I need to call a meeting of my board of directors to get some advice? How are my finances looking in relation to my goal of doing summer stock theatre next year? Should I spend some time following up with those actors who came to my recent workshop to see if they need some career coaching? How much research will I need to do in order to start recording this new audiobook project? Should I make plans to visit one of the art museums this weekend and take in a little food for the soul? The list is never-ending, continually evolving, and always at the forefront of my thoughts.

I know there's a lot to take in from this book; the ideas, concepts, and action plans are many. But don't be overwhelmed! Take it a piece at a time and add new tasks or goals as you feel ready. Develop a plan to begin working on these crucial differences that allows you to gather some quick, small successes under your belt, in order to give you the confidence to keep going. Reread it at least once a year to jog your memory and keep you focused on why you're working so diligently.   Make no mistake, being an actor is a damn hard thing succeed at, but I know that if you really take these ideas to heart and act on them, your odds of success will get a whole lot better. I wish you luck in your future endeavors, but not the dumb luck of chance...because that can come to anyone. Rather, the luck I wish you is what comes from your efforts to be in the right place at the right time with the training, confidence, and ability to seize that moment and move forward in your career. So, to quote Shakespeare, "Screw your courage to the sticking place and you shall not fail." And now... let's get started!

About the Author

ABOUT THE AUTHOR

Sean Pratt, (AEA / SAG / AFTRA), has been a professional actor in theatre, film, TV, and voice-overs for 25 years. Hailing from Oklahoma City, Sean received his BFA in acting from the College of Santa Fe in New Mexico. While living in New York City, he joined the resident acting company at the Pearl Theatre, an Off-Broadway classical repertory theatre. He has also performed principal roles at numerous regional theatres around the country; among others, the Shakespeare Theatre Company in Washington, D.C., Center Stage Theatre in Baltimore, Md., and the Actor's Shakespeare Company in Albany, N.Y.

Since moving to the Washington, D.C. area, he has worked on several major films, including Gods and Generals, Tuck Everlasting, and Iron Jawed Angels. Sean was the host of HGTV's Old Homes Restored, and has appeared in supporting roles on such television shows as Homicide, The District, and America's Most Wanted. An audiobook narrator since 1996, Sean Pratt has recorded over 660 audiobooks in almost every genre and is a six-time winner of AudioFile Magazine's "Earphones Award" and a two-time nominee for the prestigious "Audie Award."

After ten years of teaching master classes on the business of acting, Sean recently founded his company, Sean Pratt Presents, which is dedicated to teaching, motivating, and inspiring actors on a variety of topics related to the business of the Biz. He brings his classes to high schools, colleges, universities, and other groups around the country. Sean lives in Frederick, Md., with his wife, actress Shannon Parks, and their two children Noah and Olivia. For more information about Sean, go to www.SeanPrattPresents.com.

References

REFERENCES

Ericsson, K. A., Krampe, R. Th., & Tesch-Romer, C. (1993). *The role of deliberate practice in the acquisition of expert performance*. Psychological Review, 100, 363–406.

Gelb, M. (2000). *How to Think Like Leonardo da Vinci*. New York: Dell.

13621475R00069

Made in the USA
Charleston, SC
21 July 2012